A Sanctified People

LIVING WHAT WE BELIEVE

Volume 3

A Sanctified People

With Leader's Guide for SMALL GROUPS

J. Ben Wiles

ISBN: 978-1-940682-57-0

Printed in the United States of America.

TABLE OF CONTENTS

ACKNOWLEDGMENTS

I would like to express my deep gratitude to Dr. O. Wayne and Reverend Pamela R. Brewer, directors of Men's and Women's Discipleship, respectively, for seeing this vision through to its fruition. It has been a privilege to work with you on this project and I am grateful to you both for your zeal to see God's people grow into Christlikeness by the power of the Word of God and the Holy Spirit.

I also wish to express my appreciation to Dr. French Arrington, Dr. Lee Roy Martin, and Dr. Dan Tomberlin for contributing their volumes to this study. I am privileged to have been able to participate in this project with you all, and I am also privileged to know you as respected friends and colleagues in the ministry. You are all a gift to the Church.

Finally, I wish to express my love and appreciation to my wife, Pam, who has been proofreading my work since our freshman year in college and has done so in this study as well. Pam fills many roles in life—wife, mother, daughter, educator, and pastor's wife. But above all, Pam embodies the beauty of holiness. I am grateful the Lord brought us together.

The content of this volume owes much to the following works, which are offered here as a suggested reading list on the topic of sanctification and holiness:

French L. Arrington, *Exploring the Declaration of Faith* (Cleveland, TN: Pathway Press, 2003).

Dale M. Coulter, *Holiness: The Beauty of Perfection* (Cleveland, TN: Pathway Press, 2004).

R. Hollis Gause, *Living in the Spirit: The Way of Salvation* rev. ed (Cleveland, TN: CPT Press, 2009)

William M. Greathouse, *Love Made Perfect: Foundations for the Holy Life* (Kansas City, MO: Beacon Hill Press, 1997).

Chris E.W. Green, *Sanctifying Interpretation* (Cleveland, TN: CPT Press, 2015).

Henry H. Knight, *Anticipating Heaven Below: Optimism of Grace from Wesley to the Pentecostals* (Eugene, OR: Wipf and Stock Publishers, 2014).

Randy L. Maddox, *Responsible Grace: John Wesley's Practical Theology* (Nashville, TN: Abingdon Press, 1994).

Bernie A. Van De Walle, *Rethinking Holiness: A Theological Introduction* (Grand Rapids, MI: Baker Academic Press, 2017).

—J. Ben Wiles

FOREWORD

Why Living What We Believe?

Why indeed? The Living What We Believe six-volume series of small group/class studies is written and specifically developed for the purpose of making Pentecostal disciples of Jesus Christ. For those seeking to know more about living the Christ-life, there is plenty here to be learned and discussed. However, Living What We Believe (all six volumes) has much more to offer than biblical knowledge and doctrine alone. This series has been especially created to foster relational discipleship within a community of believers for the purpose of transformational life-change! Making disciples is all about developing true followers of Jesus Christ while understanding that the person and work of the Holy Spirit himself is intimately and undeniably involved in this lifelong process. It is the Holy Spirit who helps disciples become more like Jesus.

The Living What We Believe six-volume series is a complete 24-week discipleship study (though a participant or group is free to use any one volume alone, or in any order they prefer). This series both understands and is built upon the truth that only disciples make other disciples! Coming together as the body of Christ within the context of a small group is an essential and fruitful means by which Jesus' Great Commission (Matthew 28:18-20), can be fulfilled. Likewise, coming together as the body of Christ within the context of a small group is also a natural and organic means by which Jesus' Great Commandment (Matthew 22:36-40) can find a more productive fulfillment.

Over the course of the six volumes of this series, the reader/participant will be provided both biblical/doctrinal teaching based on the fourteen points of the Church of God Declaration of Faith as well as the opportunity to reflect upon and discuss the practical ramifications of living out what we believe . . . all within the relational context of small group discipleship. The general framework of the series is based upon, and generally guided by an understanding of the "Fivefold Gospel" (i.e. Jesus is our Savior, Jesus is our Sanctifier, Jesus is our Spirit-Baptizer, Jesus is our Healer, and Jesus is our coming King).

The format of the Living What We Believe series is simple, relational and structured specifically to make true disciples, as well as assisting disciple-makers to fulfill their mission. Each of the six volumes, (*A Believing People, A Saved People, A Sanctified People, A Spirit-Baptized People, A Healed People, An Expectant People*) is a four-week study with each week divided into five days. Each participant reads, reflects, and reacts to each of these days at home in his or her personal time. Each day will feature several components which enable the growth process of the disciple at a personal level:

- Search the Scripture (selected Scripture readings).
- Answer the Following Questions (reflective questions directly relevant to the Scripture selection).
- Yield to the Spirit—divided into three subsections:
  1. "Know"—relating to one's intellect (your mind).
  2. "Be"—relating to one's passion (your heart).
  3. "Do"—relating to one's behavior (your hands).
- Offer a Prayer—the conclusion of each day.

After the five daily personal interactions, the participant will join with the other members (who have likewise personally worked through the sessions) for the weekly small group session. Led by the leader/facilitator, the weekly small group meetings provide members with the time to open up, give responses, and yield to the corporate and personal leading of the Holy Spirit. The leader/facilitator does not decide the response from members, but rather asks questions and helps guide group members to the practical, behavioral outworking of what we believe as Pentecostal members of the body of Christ. Each group session is about sharing, relating, learning, and being aware of the presence of the Holy Spirit. There will be a key scripture for discussion in each group session. As you work through the studies, you will note information about the "Opening," "Prayer," "Testimony," "Discussion Questions," and the section we refer to as "Yielding to the Spirit." Group leaders will find much more very helpful information concerning both starting and leading a small group from series Assistant Editor J. Ben Wiles in the following sections of this volume. If you are a group leader/facilitator, always make sure to publicly welcome the presence of the Holy Spirit to guide, teach, convict, encourage, and unify all those who are present for the weekly group session. Remember that the ultimate benefit of the Living What We Believe discipleship series is not only the transmission of biblical/doctrinal teaching, but also it is the Spirit-led, life-transformation of men and women into healthy disciples of Jesus Christ!

As general editor and publishers of this disciple-making series, we wish to express our thanks and sincere appreciation to Assistant Editor J. Ben Wiles, whose *People of the Spirit* served as the primary template for Living What We Believe. We also wish to thank Lenae Simmons for her diligent labor in the copy editing, layout, and design of this work. Finally, we wish to convey our respect and gratitude to the scholars who authored the individual volumes:

Volume One—*A Believing People* by J. Ben Wiles

Volume Two—*A Saved People* by Lee Roy Martin

Volume Three—*A Sanctified People* by J. Ben Wiles

Volume Four—*A Spirit-Baptized People* by French L. Arrington

Volume Five—*A Healed People* by Daniel Tomberlin

Volume Six—*An Expectant People* by French L. Arrington

These authors and their insightful work and commitment to making disciples for Jesus Christ cannot be overstated.

Whether Pentecostal, evangelical, or any believer wishing to take up the cross and follow Jesus, we highly recommend all six volumes of the Living What We Believe series. If you are a disciple-maker, this series is at your service. While it can certainly be used for individual study, we highly recommend this small group experience.

O. Wayne Brewer, D.Min   Pamela R. Brewer, M.A.
Men's Discipleship   *Women's Discipleship*
   Adult Discipleship Church of God International Offices

General Editors: O. Wayne and Pamela R. Brewer
Assistant Editor: J. Ben Wiles
Chief Copy Editor, Layout, and Design: Lenae Simmons

PREFACE

How to Start a Living What We Believe Group

The following steps are important in the process of starting a group in your local church:

1. Pray and seek the leadership of the Holy Spirit to make sure He is calling you to lead a Living What We Believe group.

2. Secure permission from the pastor of your local church to lead the group.

3. Find an appropriate location that is conducive to the group encounters—either in the church facility or in a host home. Public areas such as coffee shops are not appropriate, as they would potentially hinder the group's ability to fully engage the leading of the Spirit during times of prayer.

4. Set a time and place for the first meeting.

5. Develop the group through invitation. Your goal is clear: to lead every member of the group to grow in Jesus Christ, and to discover and fulfill

God's personal call on his or her life in the power of the Holy Spirit. This is a transformation group where every member will grow and be fully involved in the discipleship process personally and by leading others in the discipleship process. Select four or, at most, five people to be in your group. Include at least one mature believer and at least one new believer. (Note: a group with four to five people is best for a study such as this one. However, if you need to have a larger group, you should not have more than 10 to 12 people).

6. Decide how you are going to handle childcare.

7. Determine the cost for the group. Group members should purchase their own copy of the student guides for each unit, unless the church has opted to make other arrangements.

8. Order materials in plenty of time to have them for the first group encounter.

9. Read through the leader's guide and acclimate yourself to the Living What We Believe discipleship process.

Keys to Successfully Leading a Small Group

1. Get to know the group members.

2. Encourage participation by everyone. Remember that discipleship and lecturing are not the same thing. You are a facilitator, and your job is to facilitate participation that leads to transformation for everyone!

    *   Communicate your expectation that everyone participates.

    *   Ask questions.

    *   Make it fulfilling so they want to return.

    *   Reduce and eliminate embarrassing and threatening situations.

    *   Protect and honor confidentiality within the group.

3. Affirming vs. Endorsing

    *   It is important that, as the leader, you affirm all the responses. You say, "Thank you, Ben," or "That's very interesting, Elizabeth." No

matter what the participants say, don't criticize their remarks. What they just said may be antagonistic to you or it may simply sound ridiculous, but don't directly criticize it. Instead, say something like, "Well, that's interesting. What do the rest of you think?" Once you, as the leader, directly disapprove of someone's comments, then some people will never speak up again. They're going to fear disapproval; once exploration stops for them, the journey does too. On the other side of the coin, while it's important to affirm all responses, avoid the temptation to endorse them. Don't say things like, "Now that's a great comment," or "I couldn't agree with you more." Such endorsements tip your hand and leave others feeling like their comments are not acceptable. Also, resist the urge to be too instructional, trying to answer everyone's questions and solve everyone's problems. Once a know-it-all person speaks up, conversation tends to shut down. You can give your own opinion, but do it in a personal and humble way. Maybe you could say, "My experience has been . . ." or "This is how I see it . . ."

4. Remember the four C's of the facilitator's role:

- **Content**—Keep the group grounded in Scripture.

- **Care**—Be sensitive to the feelings, needs, and life situations of the group members.

- **Commitment**—Demonstrate your commitment to completing the Living What We Believe process completely and thoroughly. Model your commitment by your careful preparation as the facilitator for each of the group encounters.

- **Consistency**—Follow up consistently with established schedules and routines for the group. Your consistent approach to the process will inspire the same in the participants. Also, a consistently positive attitude will go a long way to establishing a healthy environment for the group to flourish.

5. Manage difficult and challenging personalities in your group so they don't hijack the encounters.

   - The Talking Hijacker answers every question before anyone else can respond. In her book, *Help! My Small Group Has Been Hijacked!, Four Common Hijackers and ways to Respond*, Margaret Feinberg discusses helpful responses to potential small group "Hijackings."

- Your first course of action is to pull them aside in a one-on-one meeting. Thank them for their participation, but be honest with them about the need for others to participate. Consider some practical ways you could offer to help them do that (respond only to every second or third question, keep responses short, and so forth).

- Your second course of action (if the first course of action doesn't work) is to change the discussion time to a more structured format. For example, you call on people for answers.

- The Emotional Hijacker shows up every week with an emotional crisis.

  - The first course of action is to spend some one-on-one time with this person and allow him or her to emotionally unpack with you. If necessary, recommend a good counselor or a conversation with the pastor. This may alleviate the problem in the group encounter.

  - If the first course of action doesn't resolve the issue, you may need to remind the group of the task at hand, which is to work through the material, and that extra questions can be raised at the end of the session.

    o **Note**: there may be a person in your group who is just going through a difficult time and is not truly an emotional hijacker. Be open to the leading of the Holy Spirit to allow a short time of personal ministry to this person if you feel it is appropriate; then return to the material at hand for that group encounter.

6. The Leader Hijacker is a backseat driver who is constantly making suggestions about how you should lead the group.

- The first course of action is to have a one-on-one conversation with the individual. Sift through his or her comments to see if you can glean anything helpful. Sometimes, there will be good suggestions that can benefit the group. If so, mention these helpful suggestions in your conversation, which will keep the atmosphere positive. Politely ask the leader hijacker to stop doing so at the group encounters by pointing out that he/she can lead to disunity in the group.

- If the hijacker does it in another meeting, simply say, "We can talk about suggestions outside of the group encounter," then continue with the material at hand.

7. The Late Hijacker constantly walks into the group encounter late, disrupting the group and causing a loss of momentum and focus.

- Discuss the situation directly with the individual and encourage him or her to make every effort to arrive on time. If that is not possible, encourage him or her to arrive quietly and discreetly so as to not disturb the group. They should also consider waiting outside if it seems to be a particularly sensitive moment.

- If the individual continues to disrupt the group, consider privately encouraging them to find another group to join that would work better with his or her schedule.

8. Remember, you are accountable for your stewardship of the group!

- Care for them enough that you refuse to accept poor decisions or justification for inconsistent participation.

- Don't be judgmental. Address behaviors only—don't try to guess the motivation behind them.

- Pray regularly over the group.

- See yourself as a mentor/role model.

- Encourage authentic relationships and conversations in the group by modeling them. Be yourself and be real, but also be holy and be humble!

- Trust God. Whatever is accomplished is by Him and through Him and for His glory. It is His will for you and your group to succeed and He is ready

- to give you the grace to do so!

Group Covenant

Instead, speaking the truth in love, we will grow to become in every respect the mature body of him who is the head, that is, Christ. From him the whole body, joined and held together by every supporting ligament, grows and builds itself up in love, as each part does its work (Ephesians 4:15-16 NIV).

It is hoped that each individual undertaking the Living What We Believe process will experience transformation and growth in Christlikeness over the course of the experience. But individual growth alone is not enough. It must take place in the context of relationship with others of the same faith, each one building the others up so that all become mature followers of Jesus Christ and, as a result, fully functioning participants in God's plan to save creation. With that in mind, before continuing with the study, each member of the group should agree to the following covenant with one another. Please read and reflect upon the following statements and indicate your commitment to the group by signing your name at the bottom. Then each member of the Living What We Believe group should sign one another's group covenant so that everyone's copy has every signature of the group. Keep this group covenant in your book for future reference as needed.

GROUP COVENANT

PRIORITY: The group meeting will be a priority in my schedule. If I am running late or unable to attend, I will contact my group leader.

PREPAREDNESS: I realize that what I put into the lesson is what I will get out of it. Therefore, I will prepare for the lesson each week and come prepared to share.

RESPECT: Everyone has a right to his or her opinion and all questions are encouraged and respected. I will listen attentively to others without interrupting them.

CONFIDENTIALITY: Anything of a personal nature that is said in the meeting should not be repeated outside the meeting. This group is intended to be a safe place for open discussion and sharing.

HONESTY: I will strive to be real, honest, and transparent with the other group members.

SUPPORT: The mission and values of the group have my support, and I will refrain from gossip or criticism.

SIGNATURES   DATE

_____

_____

_____

_____

_____

_____

_____

_____

_____

_____

_____

_____

_____

_____

_____

_____

_____

_____

_____

_____

_____

_____

_____

_____

_____

_____

_____

_____

_____

A SANCTIFIED PEOPLE

Introduction

In this study, we continue our focus on the doctrinal statement of the Church of God known as the *Declaration of Faith*. The goal of this study is not just to learn what we believe, but to learn what it means to *live* what we believe. As Pentecostals, we embrace the view that what we believe is more than just a mental agreement to a statement of truth. It is something that should become evident in our conduct. To put it more clearly, our beliefs should lead us to *become like Jesus*!

But becoming like Jesus is not something that happens off in the distant future when we are in eternity with Him. It is something that is happening right now! The Apostle Paul wrote, "But we all, with unveiled face, beholding as in a mirror the glory of the Lord, are being transformed into the same image from glory to glory" (2 Corinthians 3:18). Note the present tense—*we are beholding,* and *we are being transformed.* Something is happening to us now that is making us more and more like Jesus. What that is, when and how it happens, and the nature of its outcome is what we will be looking at in this study you hold in your hands.

In particular, for the next four weeks we will be using statements six and seven of the Declaration of Faith to guide us in our reading of Scripture. These statements of our faith are:

"We believe in sanctification subsequent to the new birth, through faith in the blood of Christ; through the Word, and by the Holy Ghost.

We believe holiness to be God's standard of living for His people."

These two statements are intertwined in such a way that it makes it difficult for us to separate them in our dealing with them. In this study, we will talk about holiness as the goal of sanctification. And conversely, we will discuss sanctification as the process of becoming holy. In the Declaration of Faith, statement six talks about when and how sanctification happens, while statement seven addresses the issue of holiness. So keep in mind that if we are focusing on statement six, statement seven is still in the background, and vice versa.

As we begin our reading of Scripture, let us ask the Holy Spirit to guide this process in such a way that Scripture begins reading *us*. Our hope is that this study will be used by the Holy Spirit as a means of sanctifying us and calling us both individually and as the Church of God to live lives of holiness to the glory of God!

DECLARATION OF FAITH

◆◆◆◆◆◆◆

"We Believe....

In Sanctification subsequent to the new birth, through faith in the blood of Christ; through the Word, and by the Holy Ghost.

Holiness to be God's standard of living for His people."

Week 1
Day 1
What Does It Mean To Be Saved?

DECLARATION OF FAITH

"We Believe....

In Sanctification subsequent to the new birth, through faith in the blood of Christ; through the Word, and by the Holy Ghost.

Holiness to be God's standard of living for His people."

Words to Hide in Your Heart

Therefore, having these promises, beloved, let us cleanse ourselves from all filthiness of the flesh and spirit, perfecting holiness in the fear of God (2 Corinthians 7:1 NKJV).

Touching Base

As stated in the introduction, the two statements of faith in this study are closely intertwined. So this week, we are going to keep both of them in view. We will begin talking about sanctification, but we will also talk about the *goal* of sanctification, which is *holiness.*

The Greek word translated 'sanctify' is *hagiazo,* which means "to make holy, set apart, dedicate, or purify. The noun 'sanctification' is *hagiasmos* which means "holiness, or separation from profane things" (Arrington, *Christian Doctrine, vol. 2,* 230). These definitions are important for us to consider as we think about what it really means to be saved. Often, salvation is spoken of in legal terms. For example, we talk about a debt or penalty that we owe because of our sin, but are unable to pay. But Jesus paid the debt and satisfied the penalty by coming to live as a sinless man and giving His life on the cross. Because of what He accomplished for us, we are able to be made right with God. Praise the Lord, this is true! This is called *justification.*

Paul tells us in Romans 5:1-2, "Having been justified by faith, we have peace with God through our Lord Jesus Christ, through whom also we have access by faith into this grace in which we stand, and rejoice in hope of the glory of God." Because of our justification, we have been given access *into this grace.* So there is even more to what God has done for us and in us. Scripture reveals to us that, not only have we been justified, but we have been and are being sanctified. We are in the process of becoming like Christ. That process begins in the moment of our regeneration and continues throughout our life on earth as long as we are following the Lord and faithfully responding to the gracious sanctifying activity of the Holy Spirit working in our lives. One day, when we see Jesus face to face, we will no longer have to deal with sin and brokenness for all eternity. But until that time, Scripture assures us that we have been given power over sin by the indwelling Holy Spirit. Truly, the gospel is not about sin management, it is about transformation into Christlikeness in this life!

We can think of salvation as being true in a three-fold way. In justification, we are saved from the *penalty* of sin, in sanctification we are being saved from the *plague* of sin, and in our glorified eternal bodies we will be forever free from the *presence* of sin. Thanks be to God!

Read Romans 6:1-4:

> What shall we say then? Shall we continue in sin that grace may abound? Certainly not! How shall we who died to sin live any longer in it? Or do you not know that as many of us as were baptized into Christ Jesus were baptized into His death? Therefore, we were buried with

Him through baptism into death, that just as Christ was raised from the dead by the glory of the Father, even so we should walk in newness of life. For if we have been united together in the likeness of His death, certainly we also shall be in the likeness of His resurrection, knowing this, that our old man was crucified with Him, that the body of sin might be done away with, that we should no longer be slaves to sin.

Read Hebrews 13:11-12:

For the bodies of those animals, whose blood is brought into the sanctuary by the high priest for sin, are burned outside the camp. Therefore, Jesus also, that He might sanctify the people with His own blood, suffered outside the gate.

Answer the Following Questions:

1. How does Paul respond to the question of continuing in sin?

2. What does Paul say about those who have been baptized into Christ Jesus?

3. What does Christ's resurrection mean for the believer?

4. What does Paul say was crucified with Christ?

5. What has been done away with? Why?

6. Why did Jesus suffer outside the gate?

Yielding to the Spirit

—Know—

The first passage of Scripture continues from the discussion on justification that took place in Romans 5. Paul is responding to some of his opponents who suggested that if sin increases grace, then we should increase sin so there will be even more grace! Paul's response is clear—"God forbid!" Justification by grace through faith is not an excuse to live sinfully. Quite the opposite, it is a call to holiness! It is totally out of character for one who is justified to live in sin.

Human beings were created in the image of God and in their unfallen state were good—not evil (see Genesis 1:31). The plague of sin, called "original sin" has corrupted humanity's original goodness, but Christ has come to restore it. In this passage, Paul uses the term "old man" and "body of sin." These two terms refer to the same thing. It is our physical body and our emotions corrupted by original sin.

We receive more insight into what Christ has done for us in the second portion of Scripture today. The writer of Hebrews tells us that Jesus' sacrificial death on the cross was not just about us receiving forgiveness (justification)—it is about being set free from the corruption of sin (sanctification).

The good news that we read in this passage today is that as we identify ourselves with Christ in his death, that old man, corrupted by the plague of original sin, dies with Him. And as we identify with Him in His resurrection we are set free from this corruption of sin—we are sanctified!

—Be—

There is more to be said about sanctification than what has been said here. But it is important to understand the significance of this for our lives. Sanctification is not an optional "add-on" experience to justification. It is integral to what Christ has done for us. Furthermore, sanctification is not about following a list of rules, it is about being delivered *from* the corruption of original sin and delivered *to* a brand-new life of holiness.

—Do—

How have you understood your own salvation experience? Perhaps you have reflected on the forgiveness God has offered us in Christ. But what about the cleansing and deliverance made available through Christ? Many Christians are still living unnecessarily in bondage to sin. Effectively sitting in an unlocked prison cell. Whatever your experience may be, the truth of the Scripture remains the same. Christ died so we can be forgiven AND free from the penalty and power of sin.

Offer a Prayer

Lord, I come to You today to thank you for salvation. I thank You because, in Christ, provision has been made for me to be justified. But I also thank You that, in Christ, You have made it possible for me to be delivered from the corruption of sin in my life. Holy Spirit, work in my life in such a way that I continue to rely on the provision Christ has made for my sanctification and not on my own strength and will power. Help me to fully participate in the salvation made available to me in Christ. Amen.

Day 2

It All Comes Down To Love

Searching the Scripture

Read Mark 12:28-30:

> Then one of the scribes came, and having heard them reasoning together, perceiving that He had answered them well, asked Him, "Which is the first commandment of all?"

> Jesus answered him, "The first of all the commandments is 'Hear O Israel, the Lord our God, the Lord is one. And you shall love the Lord your God with all your heart, with all your soul, with all your mind, and with all your strength.' This is the first commandment. And the second, like it, is this, 'You shall love your neighbor as yourself.' There is no other commandment greater than these."

Answer the Following Questions:

1. What is the first great commandment?

2. What is the second great commandment?

3. Which other commandments are greater than these two commandments?

Yielding to the Spirit

—Know—

One could say that there are two extremes taken by Christians when speaking of the nature and goal of salvation. The first would be to focus so much on God's grace and mercy and spiritualize everything to the point that what we do in the body in this life doesn't matter at all. The other is to focus so much on following the rules that we overlook the truth of God's grace and mercy and become legalistic instead.

But here we see Jesus saying something that should challenge both views. These two commandments are "first" (i.e. greatest). In Matthew Jesus says, "on these two commandments hang all the Law and the Prophets" (Matthew 28:40). The Scripture reveals God and what it means to be God's special people. Jesus says this revelation is summed up in one word—*love*. But it is the kind of love that is expressed in the entirety of our being—who we are, what we do, and why we do it!

You might wonder what this has to do with holiness. Simply put, loving relationship is the purpose for which God created humanity. If God created us for this reason, then doing and being anything less couldn't possibly be considered *holy*.

—Be—

Being saved is more than just about the things we do or don't do. It goes much deeper, looking into *why* we are doing or not doing them. What kind of people are we and what kind of people are we becoming? This speaks to our motivations, our affections—the things that drive us. Sin has distorted us into something different than what we were created to be by God, so it isn't just our actions that are wrong. Our motivations and affections are distorted as well. The call to holiness is the call to allow God to set us right, to heal our broken and distorted selves, and to teach us once again how to love Him and love others well.

—*Do*—

It can be easy to deceive ourselves into thinking we are becoming holy based simply on the things we do that we think are spiritual—church attendance/participation, giving offerings, etc. But an excellent measure of our likeness to God is going to be found in our relationships with other people. Remember, the great commandment is loving God *and* loving others. Consider your closest relationships in your prayer time today and let the Holy Spirit show you ways He wants to transform those relationships as part of the process of you becoming holy.

Offer a Prayer

Father, I come to You today with a desire to become like You. I hear you calling me to a life of holiness and I want to be obedient and faithful. But I know I can't be that person apart from You. I ask that you grant a work of grace in my life so I may learn to love You and love others in such a way that I more clearly reflect Your image in the world. In Jesus name I pray, amen.

Day 3

Sin = Misdirected Love

Searching the Scripture

Read 1 John 2:15-17:

> Do not love the world or the things in the world. If anyone loves the world, the love of the Father is not in him. For all that is in the world—the lust of the flesh, the lust of the eyes, and the pride of life—is not of the Father but is of the world. And the world is passing away, and the lust of it; but he who does the will of God abides forever.

Read 1 John 5:19:

> We know that we are of God, and the whole world is under the sway of the wicked one.

Answer the Following Questions:

1. What are the two choices John gives as to how we are able to direct our love?

2. What are the three characteristics John gives us of the world?

3. Who currently holds sway over the world?

4. What is the ultimate end of the world? What is the ultimate end of those who do the will of God?

Yielding to the Spirit

—Know—

At first reading, this notion of not loving the world seems to contradict other places in Scripture that tell us God loves the world (John 3:16 for instance). But it isn't a contradiction at all! The word *world* here in this passage isn't talking about the creation itself. Scripture teaches us creation is good, because God declared it to be so in the creation story (Gen. 1). The word *world* in this passage (and others like it) should be understood as talking about a *world system*. Paul describes the world system as one in which God is not acknowledged and worshipped as Creator. It is a system where humanity is deceived into seeking to become gods of their own reality, making decisions about right and wrong from minds darkened by willfully ignoring what God has revealed about Himself (see Romans 1).

God gave us passions and drives as part of the created order. It is part of what He meant when He said we are made in His image. When they are directed by and toward God, they are good. But in this world system, under the sway of Satan, desires and drives are twisted to become something they were not meant to be. Those in love with the world system are driven by the urge to gratify the desires of the flesh (lust of the flesh). They desire superficial things and how they imagine them to be based only on their appearance (lust of the eye). And they are driven by the urge to fuel their pride and by gaining power and possessions in order to impress and even control others.

The Gospel tells us the Holy Spirit has empowered us to make a choice. If we love this world system and live our lives in an idolatrous relationship with it then we have chosen sin. If we choose love and fellowship with God, a choice only made possible through the person and work of Jesus the Son of God mediated to us by the Holy Spirit, then we are choosing holiness—which is what we were created for. We become like what we love. Choose wisely!

—Be—

Being saved doesn't just mean being forgiven. It means being free from bondage to the old patterns of the world system which used to enslave us. It doesn't just mean that we stop doing things we shouldn't, it means we are set free to become the person God intended for us to be when He created us. It means we receive the love of the Father and, in turn, we are able to love Him and others.

—Do—

Take time today to reflect on your life and how you are living it. Are there still ways in which you see your behaviors, your heart, and your mind are more like the world system than like God? Confess those things to the Lord and ask Him for His grace to make you more like Him and less like the world.

Offer a Prayer

Lord, I confess to You that there are areas in my life, some I am aware of and some I am not, where I need Your love and mercy to break through. I want to be free from bondage to the world system and free to love You with my whole life—every part of me. In Jesus name, amen.

Day 4

Jesus, Our Example and Goal

Searching the Scripture

Read 2 Corinthians 3:18:

> But we all, with unveiled face, beholding as in a mirror the glory of the Lord, are being transformed into the same image from glory to glory, just as by the Spirit of the Lord.

Read Ephesians 5:1-2:

> Therefore be imitators of God as dear children. And walk in love, as Christ also has loved us and given Himself for us, an offering and a sacrifice to God for a sweet-smelling aroma.

Answer the Following Questions:

1. What are we beholding as in a mirror?

2. Into what are we being transformed?

3. Who is working to accomplish this transformation in us?

4. Who are we supposed to imitate? In what way do we imitate Him?

5. How are we called to walk?

6. Who is our example for walking in this way?

Yielding to the Spirit

—Know—

In the study entitled "A Believing People," we discovered what it means to say Jesus is God. In fact, Hebrews 1:3 says Jesus is, "the brightness of His [God's] glory and the express image of His person." Jesus Himself said when we see Him we see the Father (John 14:9). Furthermore, we know God is holy (Leviticus 11:44-45; 1 Peter 1:16) and perfect (Matthew 5:48). Consequently, we can say Jesus Christ is holiness and perfection as well.

We see then that this passage of Scripture in 1 Corinthians which talks about becoming like Jesus is providing for us a picture of what sanctification looks like. It is the process of going from glory to glory, culminating in becoming like Jesus. Further, we see that this is a work which is accomplished by the Holy Spirit and not our own efforts.

But at the same time, we are called to participate in this process. We see for example, that Paul instructs the Ephesian Christians (and us) to be "imitators of God as dear children." Children love to imitate what they see (and, for parents, that can be both good and bad). As a child wants to be like the parent he or she admires and adores, we are to look to God and seek to be like Him. And we do this as children who know they are loved by the Father and who love the Father—not as laborers trying to earn their wages! But how do we imitate God? By following the example of Christ, who perfectly reveals God in the sacrificial love He has shown toward us.

—Be—

We all have people we look up to in life. They are people that embody those values we hold most dearly. These people provide an example for us to follow and a life we can aspire to live. But we can never forget that people are fallen and fallible. No one is the perfect example. We cannot measure our success in life by how much we are like our heroes. We measure our lives by how much we are becoming like Jesus in our hearts and in our conduct.

—Do—

We all have values, and we all have an image of what it looks like for those values to be lived out. Have you considered the nature of your values? What things do you think are most important in life? Now ask the Holy Spirit to show you how much your values and goals are like or unlike the example we see in the life of Jesus. Then ask the Holy Spirit to work in your life in such a way that those values begin to line up with what Jesus modeled for us.

Offer a Prayer

Lord Jesus, I thank You for the love You have shown in giving Your life to save us. You have made true life and holiness possible for us because of what You have done. Now I ask that Your saving work continue in my life. Help me to keep my focus on You as my example for how life should be lived. Your Word tells me as I do that, I will become like You. I pray for that to be true in my life more and more every day. In Your name, I pray, amen.

Day 5

A New Covenant of Holiness

Searching the Scripture

Read Jeremiah 31:31-33

"Behold the days are coming," says the Lord, "when I will make a new covenant with the house of Israel and with the house of Judah—not according to the covenant that I made with their fathers in the day that I took them by the hand to lead them out of the land of Egypt, My covenant which they broke, though I was a husband to them," says the Lord.

"But this is the covenant that I will make with the house of Israel after those days, says the Lord: I will put My law in their minds and write it on their hearts; and I will be their God, and they shall be My people."

Read Luke 22:20

Likewise He also took the cup after supper, saying, "This cup is the new covenant in My blood, which is shed for you."

Read 2 Corinthians 3:3, 5b-6

Clearly you are an epistle of Christ, ministered by us, written not with ink but by the Spirit of the living God, not on tablets of stone but on tablets of flesh, that is, of the heart...but our sufficiency is from God who also made us sufficient as ministers of the new covenant, not of the letter but of the Spirit, for the letter kills, but the Spirit gives life.

Answer the Following Questions:

1. What happened to the covenant God made with the 'fathers' of Israel?

2. Where does Jeremiah say God is going to write the new covenant?

3. What did Jesus tell His disciples about the cup when He instituted the Lord's Supper?

4. By what means and where is the new covenant written?

Yielding to the Spirit

—Know—

The reading today follows a thread that takes us from the Hebrew Scriptures through the New Testament. The focus begins on the law of God—the old covenant—which Israel failed to keep, and as a result Israel was eventually forced to leave the Promised Land and live in exile. During this time, the prophet Jeremiah wrote of a time in the future when God would make a new covenant, but this one would be different. It would not be written on tablets of stone, instead it would be written on the minds and hearts of His people.

Jesus' death, resurrection, and ascension made it possible for us to live with God in a new way. His shed blood—the giving of His life—was the seal of this new covenant relationship. And the sending of the Holy Spirit after His ascension made it possible for God's law to be written on the hearts and minds of His people. No longer are we forced to try to conform to an outward set of rules, instead we are being transformed from within as our minds and hearts are being conformed to the will of God and, consequently, our external behaviors are as well. This is the gospel—God wants to transform us into all He created us to be. And as He does so, our hearts and desires increasingly push us in the direction of holiness.

—Be—

The desire for holiness is a good thing. It is evidence of what we were created to be. But just as we are saved by grace through faith, we only become holy by grace through faith. It is a work of the Spirit of God changing our hearts and minds, resulting in greater love for God and others. It will never be a result of our own willpower.

—Do—

It is dangerous to pursue holiness by conforming to external moral standards. It is self-deception that can lead to pride and despair. Pride when we fool ourselves into thinking we have accomplished something that we really have not, and despair when we come to realize the impossibility of what we are attempting to do. Are you relying on the gracious work of the Holy Spirit to sanctify you, or are you relying on your own personal efforts? Only one way will result in true holiness!

Offer a Prayer In Your Own Words

You may wish to write your own prayer today in response to the Holy Spirit's work in your life.

Group Discussion

Key Scripture—2 Corinthians 7:1

Therefore, having these promises, beloved, let us cleanse ourselves from all filthiness of the flesh and spirit, perfecting holiness in the fear of God.

Opening—This is a time of fellowship and sharing about one another's lives.

Prayer—Ask the Lord to make His presence known and to begin the process of transformation into Christlikeness for each participant.

Testimony—Have two or three group members give a testimony of how God is at work in their lives, whether it is through their daily encounters in this study, or some other way.

Discussion Questions:

1. Sanctification and holiness are topics that often seem to confuse or divide Christians. Take some time for members of the group to share their understanding of these ideas held prior to beginning this study.

2. Discuss the idea of love as the goal of sanctification. What is the significance of Jesus saying that the command to love God and love others is greater than all the other commandments (including the moral law).

3. Have group members discuss their understanding of the concept of "sin." What is it exactly?

4. If we understand sin as the outcome of misdirected love, then how does that reveal the true meaning of sanctification? What does any of this have to do with our morality and ethics?

5. Discuss the significance of the new covenant for our sanctification. Specifically discuss the difference between the writing of the law of God on hearts and minds instead of tablets of stone. Are there ways we have tried to go back to our own version of tablets of stone in our understanding of sanctification and holiness?

Yielding to the Spirit

Group members should pair off with someone with whom they feel comfortable sharing. Take a moment to remind them of the Group Covenant, particularly the statement on confidentiality. Practice memorizing the key scripture of the week together. Then discuss any personal takeaways you would like your partner to pray about with you. Conclude this conversation by quietly praying for one another. Be attentive to the leading of the Holy Spirit in the use of spiritual gifts. If you do feel led to share something in this way, ask the group leader to come and witness what is being said. This is to provide a reliable witness for all involved.

DECLARATION OF FAITH

❖❖❖❖❖❖❖

"We Believe....

In Sanctification subsequent to the new birth, through faith in the blood of Christ; through the Word, and by the Holy Ghost."

Week 2

Day 1

Sanctification Begun

DECLARATION OF FAITH

"We Believe....

In Sanctification subsequent to the new birth, through faith in the blood of Christ; through the Word, and by the Holy Ghost."

Words to Hide in Your Heart

I beseech you therefore, brethren, by the mercies of God that you present your bodies a living sacrifice, holy, acceptable to God, which is your reasonable service. And do not be conformed to this world, but be transformed

by the renewing of your mind, that you may prove what is that good and acceptable and perfect will of God (Romans 12:1-2 NKJV).

Touching Base

This week our study on sanctification and holiness continues with a closer focus on sanctification itself. Specifically, we will work to answer questions such as, "When does sanctification happen?" "Is it instantaneous or progressive?" and "What is the believer's role in the process?" Remember that in this study, we refer to sanctification as the process of becoming holy. And, looking from the other direction, we say that holiness is the goal of sanctification. Keep these ideas in mind as we continue our study together.

We can think of the Christian as existing in three different states of being. The first state of being is the fallen state. This is prior to the conversion experience (justification, new birth, and adoption). The second state of the Christian is just after the new birth all the way to the end of this life. The third state of the Christian is the glorified state of being which we will only know in eternity. These three states of being correlate well with the three-fold view of salvation: when we are justified we are saved from the *penalty* of sin; in sanctification we are saved from the *plague* of sin; and in glorification we are saved from the *presence* of sin.

The questions we seek to answer when we talk about sanctification and holiness in this study are about the second state of the believer—between the new birth and glorification. How optimistic should we be about the effect of sanctification on the believer in this second state? Can we truly become holy in this life or does that await the life to come in our glorified state? Do we change in this second state or do we just have to "grit our teeth" and suppress the urge to sin until we are glorified?

Searching the Scripture

Read John 1:12-13:

> But as many as received Him, to them He gave the right to become children of God, to those who have believe in His name: who were born, not of blood, nor of the will of the flesh, nor of the will of man, but of God.

Read Ephesians 2:1-3:

> And you He made alive, who were dead in trespasses and sins, in which you once walked according to the course of this world, according to the prince of the power of the air, the spirit who now works in the sons of disobedience, among whom also we all conducted ourselves in the lusts of our flesh, fulfilling the desires of the flesh and of the mind, and were by nature children of wrath, just as the others.

Answer the Following Questions:

1. What has Christ given to those who receive Him?

2. How does John describe our birth? What is it? What is it not?

3. What was formerly true of those who Christ has made alive?

Yielding to the Spirit

—*Know*—

We believe in sanctification subsequent to the new birth. We will be looking at that next, but first we must acknowledge the fact that the beginnings of sanctification actually take place *in the new birth!* Justification is when God declares us to be righteous. But the new birth (also known as regeneration) is when we actually receive a new nature. We have a new nature because we have a new origin. We are no longer 'sons of disobedience' under the hypnotic sway of this world system being controlled by Satan. We are sons and daughters of God. We are a new person in Christ!

It is in this moment that the heart of stone becomes a heart of flesh as Ezekiel prophesied (Ezekiel 11:19-20) and the Spirit writes the epistle of Christ on our hearts (2 Corinthians 3:3). This is the beginning of the restoration of our ability to cooperate with the Spirit of God in the process of our transformation into Christlikeness. We are no longer slaves of sin. We are free to become all God has created us to be! Love becomes our motivation for all we say and do.

But it would be a mistake to believe this is all there is to sanctification. New birth is the moment sanctification begins. But sanctification itself occurs subsequent to the new birth.

—Be—

Scripture repeatedly uses this idea of the new birth to describe what it means to begin life with Christ. Jesus said we must come to Him as children if we are to enter into His kingdom (Matt. 18:3).

Newborn babies are radically dependent on their caregivers for everything. No matter what family an infant comes from, rich or poor, they are all the same. They bring nothing into the world and they are helpless within themselves. If we are to be born again as Scripture teaches us, then we too must allow the Holy Spirit to humble us to a place of total dependency on God for everything. Spiritual maturity doesn't mean being weaned from dependence on the Lord. It means learning to trust Him even more.

—Do—

In what ways have you tried to resist being totally dependent on the Lord? In your pursuit of righteousness and meaning in your life, are you depending fully on Him? Or are you trying to take matters into your own hands? What would it look like for you to come to Him as a child today and surrender everything to Him?

Offer a Prayer

Father, I come to You today confessing that I need to be restored to spiritual childlikeness. I have come to a place where I have tried to take matters into my own hands, do things my way in the best of my understanding. But I want to be a child again—Your child. Restore me to the freshness of my new birth, Lord. Fill my life with the joy that comes from being Your child. In Jesus' name, amen.

Day 2

Maintenance Faith

Searching the Scripture

Read Romans 6:9-14:

> Knowing that Christ, having been raised from the dead, dies no more. Death no longer has dominion over Him. For the death that He died, He died to sin once for all; but the life that He lives, He lives to God. Likewise you also, reckon yourselves to be dead indeed to sin, but alive to God in Christ Jesus our Lord.

> Therefore do not let sin reign in your mortal body, that you should obey it in its lusts. And do not present your members as instruments of unrighteousness to sin, but present yourselves to God as being alive from the dead, and your members as instruments of righteousness to God. For sin shall not have dominion over you, for you are not under law but under grace.

Read 1 John 1:9:

> If we confess our sins, He is faithful and just to forgive us our sins and to cleanse us from all unrighteousness.

Answer the Following Questions:

1. Because we have identified with Christ in His death, in what way does Paul say we are to reckon ourselves dead? And in what way are we to reckon ourselves alive?

2. What should not reign in our mortal bodies?

3. For what purpose are we to present the members of our bodies?

4. What no longer has dominion over us as believers?

5. What happens when we confess our sins to the Lord?

Yielding to the Spirit

—*Know*—

In this passage today, we see that there is an expectation for us to faithfully respond to what God has done in our new birth. The expectation is that we will "reckon ourselves dead to sin." To "reckon" means to come to a conclusion about something. By faith in what Christ's death and resurrection has accomplished in our lives through the working of the Holy Spirit, we are to conclude that we are dead to sin. Sin no longer has power over us.

But this is not a one-time thing. Our new birth requires maintenance. In the original language, the grammar of the words "do not let sin reign in your mortal body" implies that this is not a decision we make one time and then move on from there. It is an ongoing denial of the power of sin over our lives. Temptation is a never-ending assault on the Christian. We never come to a place where we cannot be tempted to sin. So daily, hourly, even minute by minute if necessary, we are to over and over again choose to not let sin reign in our bodies. And just as we were regenerated by the gracious work of the Holy Spirit, we can only maintain this life by our faithful response to the ongoing, sanctifying grace of the Holy Spirit.

One more thing needs to be said here. There will no doubt be moments when we will fail to live up to the power that has been made available to us. In a moment of weakness, we may willingly choose sin over righteousness. This is why repentance is not just for the unbeliever as part of the conversion experience. Repentance is an ongoing part of the believer's life as well. As we grow in our likeness to Christ, we will no doubt see defects in our character we were not aware of before. At other times, we may choose to "present our members as instruments of unrighteousness" and knowingly commit sin. In both cases we should confess and repent to the Lord quickly. He is quick to forgive and cleanse us again. Remember that repentance is a result of the gracious activity of the Holy Spirit in our lives. He will convict us and call us to repentance, but His voice will not be condemning.

—Be—

We saw yesterday that sanctification begins in the new birth. We are cleansed and set free from the power of sin. It no longer has control over us. But we must never forget that we have been given a free will. God gives us the choice as to how we live our lives, and He will allow our choices to be fulfilled all the way to their consequences—good or bad.

—*Do*—

Take a moment to do an inventory of your life. Are there parts of your life that you are not "reckoning yourself dead to sin?" In what ways have you "presented your members as instruments of unrighteousness?" Remember, this may not be something that manifests just in the body. Jesus even spoke to us about our mind, our hearts, our motivations. Those parts of us are also to be presented as instruments of righteousness by the grace of God.

Offer a Prayer

Father, I thank You for saving me and cleansing me because of the life, death, and resurrection of Jesus. I thank You that in saving me You also set me free from the power of sin. I ask You today to show me ways in which I may not be fully reckoning myself dead to sin's power over me. Grant me the grace to repent where necessary and help me to learn to live by faith in the gracious power of the Holy Spirit which enables me to live a sanctified life for Your glory. In Jesus' name I pray, amen.

Day 3

Fruit and More Fruit

Searching the Scripture

Read John 15:1-4:

> I am the true vine, and my Father is the vinedresser. Every branch in me that does not bear fruit He takes away; and every branch that bears fruit He prunes, that it may bear more fruit. You are already clean because of the word which I have spoken to you. Abide in Me, and I in you. As the branch cannot bear fruit of itself, unless it abides in the vine, neither can you, unless you abide in Me.

Read Galatians 5:22-23:

> But the fruit of the Spirit is love, joy, peace, longsuffering, kindness, goodness, faithfulness, gentleness, self-control. Against such there is no law.

Read Matthew 7:18-20:

> A good tree cannot bear bad fruit, nor can a bad tree bear good fruit. Every tree that does not bear good fruit is cut down and thrown into the fire. Therefore by their fruits you will know them.

Answer the Following Questions:

1. Who is the vine? Who is the vinedresser?

2. What happens to branches that do not bear fruit?

3. What must be true in order for a branch to bear fruit?

4. In what way is our true self known?

Yielding to the Spirit

—Know—

Jesus says He is the vine and we are the branches. Branches draw their life from the vine. They do not have life within themselves. But that life doesn't just keep them connected, it keeps them alive. And the way one knows a branch is alive is that it bears fruit.

This way of looking at sanctification shows us there is a process involved in becoming fruit bearers. The branch abides in the vine. We enter into relationship with Christ in our conversion. As we continue to live with Him in this way, the result will be that our lives will bear fruit. Of course, this isn't the kind of fruit you eat, it is the fruit of character which glorifies God. But notice what happens when the Christian bears fruit. The vinedresser will prune it so it can bear *more fruit*. This is a picture of the process of sanctification by which we are becoming more and more like Christ.

Paul offers a helpful addition to this conversation when he offers a description of the fruit of the Spirit. If the Christian is faithful to respond to the Holy Spirit's work in his or her life, these attributes will become more and more evident. Notice they are not so much about external behaviors as they are internal attitudes and motivations. But at the same time, Paul is clear that the visible outcome of this fruit will produce behaviors which honor God's moral law.

The lesson is that when God heals our hearts and minds from the corruption of sin, the changes will manifest in holiness both "inside and out." The motivation for our behaviors will be a result of the fruit of the Spirit being cultivated in our lives. Who we really are will be known by the fruit of our lives—good or bad. And the quality of the fruit of our lives is based on our willingness to respond faithfully to the Holy Spirit's sanctifying activity in our lives.

The normal Christian life is this—right now we are being transformed into people who are more and more like Jesus. How is that possible? It is because of the sanctifying work of the Holy Spirit that *love for God and love for others* increasingly becomes our natural response to the situations we face in this life. This is holiness.

—Be—

We have already said the goal of sanctification is to be like Christ or, put another way, the goal of sanctification is holiness. It is this forward-focused aspect of sanctification where we speak of the process of growth in sanctifying grace. This growth is what is in view in these two passages of Scripture today.

There is a well-known quote from C.S. Lewis in his book *Mere Christianity* that sheds light on this idea:

> Every time you make a choice you are turning the central part of you, the part of you that chooses, into something a little different from what it was before. And taking your life as a whole, with all your innumerable choices, all your life long you are slowly turning this central thing into a heavenly creature or into a hellish creature.

Prior to our new birth, when we were slaves to sin, our choices revealed what we were becoming. Our eternal destiny had already begun breaking into our life in this present age in the "hellish" fruit we were bearing (see Galatians 5:19-21). In the same way, there are two sides to sanctification—what has been accomplished for us in the past and what is being accomplished in us now and going into the future. We often speak of what we are *free from*. But being free from one thing means we are *free to be and do another thing*. This is an important part of the discussion of sanctification. What are we *becoming?* Jesus said the answer to that question is going to be found in observing the fruit of our lives (Matthew 7:18-20)

—Do—

What is the fruit of your life? Does it match up to what Paul describes in Galatians 5? Or is it something else? Remember, your fruit reveals a great deal about who you really are and what you are becoming. Being sanctified is bearing spiritual fruit, and being pruned to bear even more spiritual fruit. But that doesn't come from our efforts alone. It comes from abiding in Christ, spending time with Him in prayer, in His word, and making full use of everything He gives to us for the purpose of our transformation into Christlikeness—our sanctification.

Offer a Prayer

Lord, I truly want to be like You and I know this is Your will for my life. I also know that You are at work in my life to make this possible. I need You to change me from the inside out, to change the very desires and motivations of my life. Heal my heart and mind where they have been distorted by the corruption of sin in this world. I surrender myself to Your sanctifying grace. Even though the cares of this life work against it at times, help me to abide in You always. I know by doing this, I will bear fruit that glorifies God.

Day 4

Keep Your Eye On The Goal

Searching the Scripture

Read Hebrews 12:1-3:

> Therefore we also, since we are surrounded by so great a cloud of witnesses, let us lay aside every weight, and the sin which so easily ensnares us, and let us run with endurance the race that is set before us, looking unto Jesus, the author and finisher of our faith, who for the joy that was set before Him endured the cross, despising the shame, and has set down at the right hand of the throne of God. For consider Him who endured such hostility from sinners against Himself, lest you become weary and discouraged in your souls.

Answer the Following Questions:

1. What surrounds us?

2. What are we to lay aside?

3. How are we supposed to run?

4. Who are we to be looking toward?

5. What did Jesus endure? Why did He endure it?

6. What do we need to do when we start to get weary and discouraged in our souls?

Yielding to the Spirit

—*Know*—

Sanctification is a lifelong process of increasingly being conformed to Christlikeness. The Scripture reading today imagines this as a long-distance race. This is not a race we run alone. There are others—a great cloud of witnesses the writer calls them. This cloud of witnesses should not be understood as saints of old watching us from Heaven. Instead, their lives are a witness to us of God's grace and mercy as we read about them on the pages of Scripture. Hebrews 11 is dedicated to talking about some of these faithful witnesses. We also experience this as we hear testimonies of our brothers and sisters in the Lord when they share the ways that God has strengthened them on the race they are running. This is how we encourage one another, and why it is important for us to come together regularly, even more so as we near the return of the Lord (Hebrews 10:25).

Another important thing we do is to lighten our load. This is what it looks like for us to cooperate with the sanctifying work of the Holy Spirit as He reveals to us and convicts us of things that are unlike Jesus which we are carrying with us. We may not even realize they are sin until they begin to entangle us.

The writer tells us to run the race with endurance. We have to pace ourselves to do this. If a distance runner starts out running too fast, then it may be difficult to finish the race. We need to have a pace that will allow us to finish. The Holy Spirit will set that pace for us. We just need to make sure we don't get ahead of Him or behind Him. He knows when we need to push a little harder and He knows when we need to rest. Following His lead in this way is crucial to finishing our race successfully.

There will be times that we grow weary. In a long-distance race there are times when the runner is hit with an injury, or maybe deals with difficult weather conditions, or difficult terrain. But if we keep our eyes on Jesus, we see the one who has run this race before us and did it successfully. He understands what we face and is ready to help us when we call out to Him. And one day when we cross the finish line, He will be there to greet us and we will hear Him say, "well done!"

—Be—

If we are to complete this race successfully, it is going to take focus. In Philippians 3, Paul said, "I press toward the goal for the prize of the upward call of God in Christ Jesus." The term he uses there implies every fiber of his being is focused on the goal of perfect fellowship with Christ forever. That has to be true of us as well.

In this passage, we are told keep our eyes on Jesus who went the distance for us because He knew that ahead of Him was the joy of fulfilling the Father's will and making our salvation possible. When we are busy keeping our eyes on Jesus, we are not able to compare ourselves with other people. We can encourage them on to good works in their journey of sanctification. But in the end, Jesus is the focus of our attention. He is the source of our strength and the goal of our transformation.

—Do—

Focus. Pace. Lightening our load. All of these ideas have been a part of today's reading. How are you doing in these areas? Are you keeping your eyes on Jesus, or do you find yourself making comparisons with other people? Are you pacing yourself? Are you making sure you stay in step with the Holy Spirit and getting the resources you need to finish strong? Are you in community with other believers who are running the race, so you can be encouraged and be an encouragement to others? What is one thing you need to do today to cooperate with the Holy Spirit's sanctifying work in your life that will better enable you to finish this race well?

Offer a Prayer

Father, I recognize I am running this long-distance race the Scripture is speaking about today. I also know that unless I lean on You completely, I won't be able to finish well. Help me to follow the leading of the Holy Spirit, not getting ahead or behind. And help me to keep my eyes on Jesus, so I don't make the mistake of comparing myself with other people. I want to be encouraged by and also be an encouragement to those around me as we all keep our eyes on the author and finisher of our faith—Jesus Christ.

Day 5

Glorification

Searching the Scripture

Read 1 John 3:1-3

> Behold what manner of love the Father has bestowed on us, that we should be called children of God! Therefore the world does not know us, because it did not know Him. Beloved, now we are children of God; and it has not yet been revealed what we shall be, but we know that when He is revealed, we shall be like Him, for we shall see Him as He is. And everyone who has this hope in Him purifies Himself, just as He is pure.

Answer the Following Questions:

1. What are we called because of the love the Father has bestowed on us?

2. When is it true that we are children of God?

3. What about us has not yet been revealed?

4. What will be true about us when we see God as He is?

5. What is true of everyone who has this hope?

Yielding to the Spirit

—Know—

As mentioned in the introduction this week, our focus has been primarily on the second state of being as humans, namely what happens to us between the new birth and our resurrection. We have seen sanctification begin in the new birth, and we have seen sanctification continue as growth in Christlikeness. Sanctification is a work of God, but requires our faithful participation as the Spirit enables us to choose righteousness. Over time, as we abide in Christ we bear more and more fruit and we become more and more like Him.

But there is a limit to how far that will go in this life. As long as we exist in these mortal bodies, there is a distance between us and perfect expression of the image of God that cannot be closed. But after the resurrection when we are given glorified bodies, that gap will be closed, and the process of sanctification will culminate in what we call "glorification."

The portion of Scripture in focus today is one of several which describes this state of being. When we see Christ as He truly is (as opposed to what Paul describes as looking through a mirror dimly which is our current situation), then we will be like Him. This event is in the future for those who have been born again by grace through faith in Christ.

But at the same time in this Scripture there is a sense that this is already happening. John says *now* we are children of God, but it has not yet been revealed what we shall be. We know Christ now, but *then* we will see Him as He is, and we will be fully transformed into His likeness. We will be glorified because we have faithfully responded to the sanctifying grace of the Holy Spirit.

—*Be*—

There is a tension here which theologians call the "now/not yet." *Now* we are children of God, but what we really are has *not yet* been revealed. *Now* we know Jesus, but we do *not yet* know Him as He truly is.

It is important for us to hold onto this tension. It helps us realize that in this life, there is always some way we are unlike Christ, thus we are not entirely sanctified. There is no room for pride or comparison to others. None of us have arrived! But at the same time, there is a *now* component to sanctification which has been the focus of this study. As we purify ourselves by our faithful response to the sanctifying grace of the Holy Spirit, we increasingly become like Jesus *now*.

—*Do*—

Over and over again in this study we refer to our "faithful response to the sanctifying grace of the Holy Spirit." This is an important idea. Our very ability to respond is because of the Holy Spirit's gracious activity in the first place. And our faithful response empowered by the Spirit is a critical part of our sanctification. Are you responding faithfully to all the Holy Spirit is doing in your life at the moment? Today, take time to listen to the Holy Spirit for the answer to that question. Then write and offer your own prayer in response.

Offer a Prayer In Your Own Words

You may wish to write your prayer in this space.

Group Discussion

Key Scripture— Romans 12:1-2

> I beseech you therefore, brethren, by the mercies of God, that you present your bodies a living sacrifice, holy, acceptable to God, which is your reasonable service. And do not be conformed to this world, but be transformed by the renewing of your mind, that you may prove what is that good and acceptable and perfect will of God.

Opening—This is a time of fellowship and sharing about one another's lives.

Prayer—Ask the Lord to make His presence known and to begin the process of transformation into Christlikeness for each participant.

Testimony—Have two or three group members give a testimony of how God is at work in their lives, whether it is through their daily encounters in this study, or some other way.

Discussion Questions:

1. Discuss what ideas about sanctification and holiness have been reinforced so far in this study. In other words, what has not changed about what individuals believe about the topic?

2. Discuss new insights which have been gained about the topic of sanctification and holiness this week.

3. Discuss the difference between new birth and sanctification. Have a couple of group members share testimonies of their experiences of how this has worked out in their lives.

4. Discuss agreement/disagreement with this idea as a group: "Instead of talking about sanctification in terms of the eradication of sin, we should talk about it in terms of becoming more and more like Christ."

5. Discuss the idea of maintaining the now/not yet tension of sanctification. What are the implications of resolving that tension on the side of "not yet?" What are the implications of resolving the tension on the side of "now?"

Yielding to the Spirit

Group members should pair off with someone with whom they feel comfortable sharing. Take a moment to remind them of the Group Covenant, particularly the statement on confidentiality. Practice memorizing the key scripture of the week with one another. Then discuss any personal takeaways that you would like your partner to pray about with you. Conclude this conversation by quietly praying for one another. Be attentive to the leading of the Holy Spirit in the use of spiritual gifts. If you do feel led to share something in this way, ask the group leader to come and witness what is being said. This is to provide a reliable witness for all involved.

DECLARATION OF FAITH

◆ ◆ ◆ ◆ ◆ ◆ ◆

"*We Believe….*

In Sanctification subsequent to the new birth, through faith in the blood of Christ; through the Word, and by the Holy Ghost."

Week 3

Day 1

Understanding Grace

DECLARATION OF FAITH

"*We Believe....*

In Sanctification subsequent to the new birth, through faith in the blood of Christ; through the Word, and by the Holy Ghost."

Words to Hide in Your Heart

Therefore, my beloved, as you have always obeyed, not as in my presence only, but now much more in my absence, work out your own salvation with fear and trembling; for it is God who works in you both to will and to do for His good pleasure (Philippians 2:12-13).

Touching Base

The first two weeks of this study focused on the "what" and "when" aspects of sanctification and holiness. We have seen that sanctification is the process of becoming holy, or conversely, holiness is the outcome of sanctification. Furthermore, we have discovered that another term for holiness is Christlikeness. Holiness is the shape of a life that is motivated by love for God and love for others, as Christ Himself perfectly lived out in His incarnate form. We will never become divine because we are created beings! But sanctification transforms us into the *likeness* of the divine Savior. That transformation is happening in this life and will culminate in our glorification in the life to come. And just as we are justified by the empowering grace of God through faith in Jesus Christ, we are sanctified by the empowering grace of God through faith in Jesus Christ. We can't make it happen ourselves. It only happens as we submit and faithfully respond to the work of the Holy Spirit in our lives.

That brings us to the topic in focus for this week. We move on from the "what" and "when" of sanctification and holiness to a closer look at the "how" aspect. We will begin this week by a closer focus on what we actually mean when we say "grace." And then we will consider ways in which sanctifying grace is made available to us.

The term we will use to describe such things is "means of grace." God has not left our sanctification to random chance. He has provided means of grace as ways we can be shaped into Christlikeness as we participate in the Christian life with others. The dual basis for these means of grace is the Word of God and the Holy Spirit.

Searching the Scripture

Read 1 Peter 5:10

> But may the God of all grace, who called us to His eternal glory by Christ Jesus, after you have suffered a while, perfect, establish, strengthen, and settle you.

Read Romans 5:1-2

> Therefore, having been justified by faith, we have peace with God through our Lord Jesus Christ, through whom also we have access by faith into this grace in which we stand, and rejoice in hope of the glory of God.

Answer the Following Questions:

1. How does Peter refer to God?

   God of all Grace

2. What will God do for these believers after they have suffered awhile?

3. According to Paul in Romans, how have we been justified?

    By faith

4. What do we now have with God through Christ as a result of our justification?

    Peace

5. What access are we given through our Lord Jesus Christ?

    Grace

6. What causes us to rejoice?

Yielding to the Spirit

—*Know*—

An important idea that has been hinted at throughout this study is the notion of grace. What exactly is grace? Typically, the answer given to this question is, "grace is the unmerited favor of God." And that is certainly true. We don't deserve God's favor by our own efforts at becoming worthy. We are made worthy by God's own gracious activity in our lives. But there is more to grace than this.

The term for grace in the New Testament is *charis*. There are two basic meanings of this word. First, we understand grace/*charis* to be what is made available to us in our conversion based on the birth, life, death, and resurrection of Jesus. As Paul says, "For by grace you have been saved through faith, and that not of yourselves; it is the gift of God, not of works, lest any man should boast" (Ephesians 2:8-9).

But another meaning for grace/*charis* is God's power and presence at work in our lives enabling us to be who God has called us to be and do what God has called us to do. That is what Paul is referring to in Romans 5:2 when he notes that we have access *into this grace in which we stand.* There is more to grace than God's unmerited favor to save us.

We stand in *charis,* and because of Christ we have access into this same *charis.* The manifestation of the Holy Spirit includes "gifts of grace" (*charismata*) that edify the body of Christ in various ways (See for example Romans 12:6; 1 Corinthians 12:4-11; 1 Peter 4:10; Ephesians 3:8) which are aids in our sanctification as well as empowering for fulfillment of the mission of God. In this sense, all the means of sanctifying grace are made available to us because of Christ and by the work of the Holy Spirit.

—Be—

The grace of God comes to us in many different ways. It comes as a result of God's favor because we certainly are not worthy within ourselves or by our own efforts. We are only made worthy because of what has been done for us in Jesus Christ. However, God's grace does not exclude our effort! Christian writer Dallas Willard once said that "Grace is not opposed to effort. Grace is opposed to earning." By its very definition, we understand we can't *earn* grace. But as God enables us by His grace, we are called to respond faithfully to Him in such a way that by our words and actions we come into agreement with the prayer our Lord taught us to pray, "Your kingdom come, Your will be done, on earth as it is in heaven."

—Do—

It is not just unbelievers that need God's grace. It is Christians. Perhaps Christians need it even more. Because all that God has called us to do and be require His enabling power and presence—in other words, His grace! Paul said in 2 Corinthians 12:9 that instead of boasting in his strengths and accomplishments, he would rather boast in his weakness. He had learned a lesson we all need to remember—when we are weak, the Lord is strong. And His grace is sufficient for us. Are you relying on your strengths? Or are you fully relying on God's grace for all things in your life?

Offer a Prayer

Father, I acknowledge there may be times when I have relied on my strengths, insights, and abilities in my endeavors for You in this life. Forgive me for those times when I have acted as if I did not need Your grace. Teach me to rely on You for all things in my life. Like Paul, rather than boast in my strengths, help me to boldly confess my need for your grace in all things.

Day 2

Sanctified By The Word Of God

Searching the Scripture

Read Psalm 119:10-11

> With my whole heart I have sought You; Oh, let me not wander from Your commandments! Your word have I hidden in my heart, That I might not sin against You.

Read John 17:14-17

> I have given them Your word; and the world has hated them because they are not of the world, just as I am not of the world. I do not pray that You should take them out of the world, but that You should keep them from the evil one. They are not of the world, just as I am not of the world. Sanctify them by your truth. Your word is truth.

Answer the Following Questions:

1. Where has the psalmist hidden God's Word? Heart
   Why has he done so? not sin against God

2. What has Jesus given the disciples?

   Word

3. Why does the world hate Jesus' disciples?

   They are not of the world

4. What is Jesus *not asking* the Father to do? What is He asking the Father to do instead of this?

   Take them out of the world

5. How does Jesus pray for the disciples to be sanctified?

6. What is the truth?

Yielding to the Spirit

—Know—

We know that sanctification is only made possible because of the birth, life, death, resurrection, and ascension of Jesus. Everything that we are and everything that we will become is based on the supreme sacrifice of the Son of God. Our focus this week is the means by which the grace of God actually makes it possible for us to experience sanctification. One way the Holy Spirit works to sanctify us is through the Word of God.

The New Testament portion of Scripture we read today is from a larger passage in John 17, known as the "High Priestly Prayer." We are given a front row seat to hear Jesus interceding for His disciples and for all who would eventually become part of His Church. That includes us! In this prayer He asks the Father to sanctify His disciples by the truth. Then He expounds on this by saying "Your word is truth" (v.17).

Of course, we believe the Bible to be the inspired, infallible, authoritative Word of God. But words alone do not convey sanctifying grace. There is nothing magical about the words on the pages of the Bible. This is why we use the term "means of grace." As we read Scripture, we encounter a Holy God. We see the lengths that He has gone to redeem lost humanity. We hear His call to holiness of life. We hear His wisdom. And in hearing such things through the pages of Scripture we are challenged in our own perspectives. By reading Scripture with the illumination of the Holy Spirit we learn who God is, what God is doing, and consequently we learn who we are meant to be and how God is working in our lives and in all of creation to get us there. We experience this sanctifying grace in our own personal reading of Scripture, and we also experience this as we hear the word preached and taught by faithful servants of the Lord who are gifted to do so. Like the psalmist, we hide God's words in our heart that we might not sin against Him.

—Be—

We must be sure to understand that reading Scripture is not just about learning facts and insights about the things of God. There is something much more powerful at work. Dr. Chris Green states it well when he says,

> The Scripture does not merely *tell* about salvation. By the Spirit's grace, the Scripture *works* salvation, renewing our vision of the world by transforming us at the depths of our being. So transformed, we begin to discover our place in the mission of God entrusted

to the church, and to bring his goodness and justice to bear in the lives of our neighbors and enemies.

—Do—

In what ways have you submitted your life to the discipline of reading Scripture? Are you consistently participating in the life of a local church, hearing the word preached and taught by gifted men and women? Are you reading Scripture in your own personal devotional life? What is one thing you can do this week that would better position you to experience the Spirit's sanctifying grace through the means of God's Word?

Offer a Prayer

Father, I pray that You would help me to discover ways that I can be sanctified by the truth of Scripture. Show me how to carve out time in my schedule to be a faithful hearer of Your word both in my personal devotional time and as part of a vibrant local church that faithfully preaches and teaches Your Word. With the psalmist, I want to be able to say that I have hidden Your word in my heart that I might not sin against You. By my hearing of Your Word, transform me more and more into the image of Your Son, Jesus. It is in His name I pray, amen.

Day 3

Sanctified by Corporate Worship

Searching the Scripture

Read Ephesians 4:11-16

And He Himself gave some to be apostles, some prophets, some evangelists, and some pastors and teachers, for the equipping of the saints for the work of ministry, for the edifying of the body of Christ, till we all come to the unity of the faith and of the knowledge of the Son of God, to a perfect man, to the measure of the stature of the fullness of Christ; that we should no longer be carried about with every wind of doctrine, by the trickery of men, in the cunning craftiness of deceitful plotting, but, speaking the truth in love, may grow up in all things into Him who is the head—Christ—from whom the whole body, joined and knit together by what every joint supplies, according to the effective working by which every part does its share, causes growth of the body for the edifying of itself in love.

Read Hebrews 10:25

Not forsaking the assembling of ourselves together, as is the manner of some, but exhorting one another, and so much the more as you see the Day approaching.

Answer the Following Questions:

1. For what purpose did Jesus give apostles, prophets, evangelists, pastors, and teachers to the church?

2. What goals does Paul list for Christians as a result of the ministry of the church?

3. What does Christ enable the body (the Church) to do for itself?

Grow

4. How is the body of Christ held together?

Love

5. What is happening as the body of Christ is building itself up?

Growing

6. What does effective working look like in the body of Christ?

Working together

7. What should we be doing for one another when we assemble as the church?

Yielding to the Spirit

—Know—

Today's reading from Ephesians pictures a local church that is functioning in a healthy way. First of all, there is recognition of the various kinds of ministry gifts that God gives to the church—apostles, prophets, evangelists, pastors and teachers. The function of these gifts is to equip the saints—that is all of us—for the work of ministry and for building up the body of Christ— which is another term for the Church.

Paul tells us that the outcome of this kind of leadership in the church results in Christians who are no longer infants. We are called to grow up in unity in Christ and become contributing members of the Church. We do this by using our gifts to strengthen and encourage our brothers and sisters in the local church, and at the same time we allow them to do the same for us. Anyone that thinks they can bring something to the table and not take something away from it for themselves is going to end up empty and hollow. We give and receive from one another and from the Lord in the body of Christ. And notice the outcome of this ministry to one another—the body grows and is built up in love. This is the process of sanctification!

This is why the writer of Hebrews cautions us to not take this gathering of Christians for granted. As the return of the Lord draws nearer, it is even more important that we gather together to build one another up in this way. When we gather in corporate worship, the Holy Spirit is at work sanctifying us individually as well as corporately as we use our gifts of grace, our *charismata*, to build up and encourage one another in our journey toward holiness.

—Be—

Paul presents a beautiful picture of unity in this passage and others like it. But it is important to remember that unity does not require uniformity. As a matter of fact, unity is most beautiful and powerful when it exists in diversity. All of God's children have been given gifts of grace to be used for building up and encouraging one another. But not all of us have the same gift. We are each unique individuals with differing perspectives, strengths, weaknesses, and giftedness. If we are going to benefit from corporate worship and participation in the local church in a way God intends, we will have to learn to navigate those differences. But even the process of doing this is an avenue by which we experience the sanctifying grace of God.

—Do—

For various reasons, some individuals have decided that they don't want or need to participate in a local church any longer. Some have decided they can experience God on their own rather than having to navigate the challenges of doing life with a diverse group of Christians. But that is not an option given to us in Scripture.

No local church is going to be perfect. But it is still the object of Christ's affection and a means by which the Holy Spirit ministers sanctifying grace to us. Just being a member isn't enough. You have to show up, receive from the gifts of others, and share the gifts the Spirit has given to you. Are you participating faithfully in a local church? How can you engage more fully in what the Spirit is doing there? Perhaps you can talk to a pastor or another church leader about this part of the Spirit's sanctifying work in your life.

Offer a Prayer

Lord, I recognize that your Church is the place where You have given gifts in order to mature your people. Help me to learn to love Your Church more. Work in my heart in such a way that I am able to fully participate in what You are doing in the local church—both benefiting from and contributing to what is happening there in the power of the Holy Spirit. And especially grant me the grace to appreciate those who are different from me and to learn how You might be working through them to make me more like You. In Jesus name, amen.

Day 4

Sanctified by Sacred Signs

Searching the Scripture

Read Genesis 1:31a
> Then God saw everything that He had made, and indeed it was very good.

Read Romans 8:20-22
> For the creation was subjected to futility, not willingly, but because of Him who subjected it in hope; because the creation itself also will be delivered from the bondage of corruption into the glorious liberty of the children of God. For we know that the whole creation groans and labors with birth pangs together until now.

Read Colossians 1:15-20
> He is the image of the invisible God, the firstborn over all creation. For by Him all things were created that are in heaven and that are on earth, visible and invisible, whether thrones or dominion or principalities or powers. All things were created through Him and for Him. And He is before all things, and in Him all things consist. And He is the head of the body, the church, who is the beginning, the firstborn from the dead, that in all things He may have the preeminence. For it pleased the Father

that in Him all the fullness should dwell, and by Him to reconcile all things to Himself, by Him, whether things on earth or things in heaven, having made peace through the blood of His cross.

Answer the Following Questions:

1. What was God's opinion concerning everything that He had made?

    Very Good

2. What happened to creation as a result of the Fall?

3. What will creation ultimately be delivered from in the future?

4. By Whom were all things created?

    God

5. What is being reconciled to the Father through Jesus?

    all things

Yielding to the Spirit

—*Know*—

Our reading today takes us back to the very beginning of the story of God. We need to do this so we can be reminded that matter in itself is not evil. We know this because everything that God has created was declared by Him to be "good." God used the material He created to form humanity out of the dust of the earth and breathed His Spirit into him, and "man became a living soul." As a result of the introduction of sin into the relationship between God and humanity, creation itself was subjected to the curse which resulted in what Paul calls "futility" (translated "frustration" in the NIV). But we also see in Scripture that God is redeeming *all things* in Christ by His cross. All things includes everything that was created in heaven or on earth. As Christians experience sanctification, we are experiencing a foretaste of future full salvation, in other words our glorification, in the present. In the same way, God is sanctifying this present material world in advance of the day in which it will be glorified in the New Heaven and New Earth (see Revelation 21).

Because of this, we know God desires to use material things as means by which we can experience His sanctifying grace. Pentecostalism at its very heart is a very physical/sensory type of encounter with God. We anoint with oil and pray with the laying on of hands for the sick or for purposes of anointing people for ministry. We believe in speaking in tongues as evidence of the Holy Spirit's empowering presence in our lives. The book of Acts speaks about prayer cloths that had touched Paul being sent out to the sick who in turn experienced healing from disease and demonization (Acts 19:11-12). Prayer cloths are not uncommon in the Pentecostal worship experience today!

Other ways Pentecostals experience the presence and power of the Holy Spirit are through water baptism, the Lord's Supper, and footwashing. These sacred signs will be covered in much more detail in a later volume of this series. In no way do Pentecostals see these sacred signs as magical. But Pentecostals do believe the Holy Spirit blesses us as we participate in them with an active faith and in obedience to Christ.

There is an even deeper truth here. God has demonstrated His desire to minister His grace to us by means of material things. The ultimate way He has done this is through the incarnation of Christ. God Himself took on a human body, just like ours, and came to save lost humanity and restore all things back to Himself. If material was inherently evil, He wouldn't have done that. And if He came as a human, why would we not believe He allows us to physically encounter Him through such things as bread, water, and the fruit of the vine? Indeed, Scripture teaches us that He does this very thing. And by participating in these sacred signs with an active faith, we find yet another way the Holy Spirit makes sanctifying grace available to God's people.

—Be—

An openness to sacred signs as a means of sanctifying grace is an important part of our growth as Christians. We need to understand God doesn't artificially separate spiritual from physical. The "spiritual things" we believe and do should also manifest in our physical bodies. In the same way, God comes to us at times in spiritual revelations, dreams, and visions. But He also comes to us in common things such as water or bread.

It is interesting to note that Scripture refers to the Church in terms of ordinary, everyday things—salt, light, a human body, a family, a house, and a temple made with living stones. The Church is made up of common, everyday people who have been cleansed and are being sanctified, filled with the Spirit of God and sent out into the world to share the good news of Jesus. If you think about it, the Church itself is a sacred sign by which the lost can experience the saving grace of Jesus.

—Do—

It is important for Christians to avail themselves of any means the Holy Spirit chooses to convey His sanctifying grace to them. At any given time, the Holy Spirit may work through a powerful worship service filled with exuberant singing, the manifestation of spiritual gifts, and powerful preaching. Those times are important to us as Pentecostal people! But it should be equally important, and we should be equally faith-filled and expectant when the Holy Spirit chooses sacred signs like water baptism, the Lord's Supper, and footwashing as means of sanctifying grace.

Offer a Prayer

Lord, I thank You that You use seemingly ordinary things as a means of sanctifying grace in my life. I am grateful that You have invited me to participate in the Lord's Supper, water baptism, and footwashing as well as other material means of grace You may sovereignly choose to utilize to strengthen me on this journey to holiness. Help me not to take those opportunities for granted, and instead to approach them with an expectancy of an encounter with the sanctifying Holy Spirit.

Day 5

"All Things" A Means of Grace

Searching the Scripture

Read Romans 8:28-29

> And we know that all things work together for good to those who love God, to those who are the called according to His purpose. For whom He foreknew, He also predestined to be conformed to the image of His Son, that He might be the firstborn among many brethren.

Read Philippians 3:10-11

> That I may know Him and the power of His resurrection, and the fellowship of His sufferings, being conformed to His death, if, by any means, I may attain to the resurrection from the dead.

Answer the Following Questions:

1. What things work together for good to those who love God?

   all things

2. What is true about those who God foreknew?

3. In what two ways does Paul specify He wants to know Christ?

4. To what is Paul being conformed?

5. What is Paul wanting to attain?

Yielding to the Spirit

—Know—

This week's study has been about the various ways the Holy Spirit makes sanctifying grace available to us. We saw this happening through the reading and hearing of Scripture, participation in the life of a local church, and through visible sacred signs such as communion or footwashing. But today, we are going to widen our perspective of ways the Spirit might choose to work to include *all things*.

Romans 8:28 is an oft-quoted Scripture. Sadly, it is also an often misused Scripture. Instead of the meaning which is conveyed in the context of this verse, the "good" that Paul writes about is often mistaken to mean our comfort in this life. But that is not what is in view here.

Romans 8 is a culmination of Paul's presentation of the gospel to the church at Rome. Here we see the goal of God's saving activity is to sanctify and restore His creation, culminating in the glorification of the "sons and daughters of God" in the New Heaven and New Earth. In Romans 8:28-29, Paul is encouraging his hearers that no matter what they are going through in life, the Lord is able to use it for that purpose—our glorification. In other words, the Holy Spirit can turn any situation—good or bad—into a means whereby we can experience His sanctifying grace! This is not about things always working out the way we want. It is about things working out according to God's wonderful plan. Holiness!

This is why Paul says his goal is simply to know Christ—to be in close relationship with Him. And that includes knowing Him in the power of his resurrection and the fellowship of His sufferings. In all aspects of our life—at home, at work, at play, at church—whether in moments of triumph or moments of sorrow, the Holy Spirit can use the circumstances to sanctify God's people. The glorification of the sons and daughters of God is His ultimate goal!

—Be—

Life can seem like a roller coaster. Up one day and down the next. We have days when it feels like everything is going our way, and then we have days when it seems that everything is falling apart. But Scripture tells us that we should give thanks in everything— everything, not just good things (1 Thessalonians 5:18). We are told to "rejoice always"—not just when things are going our way (Philippians 4:4). The only way we can do these things is if we believe the truth we read in Romans 8:28-29.

—*Do*—

As we come to the conclusion of another week of study, today is a good day to reflect on what you have read thus far. Consider the various ways the Holy Spirit is at work in your life. How might the Holy Spirit be using various situations as a means of sanctifying grace? How will you respond?

Offer a Prayer

Lord, I am grateful You are my Shepherd. You take care of my needs. You give me opportunities to rest in times of peace and plenty. You are sanctifying me and leading me into a life of holiness so that Your name will be glorified through me. Even though I find myself walking through difficult seasons, seasons in which I may even face death, I don't have to be afraid because I know I am never alone. You are with me. Your Spirit will guide me and correct me as needed. Because of You, I am able to experience abundance in the presence of those who would enjoy seeing me suffer. The anointing of the Holy Spirit overflows in my life. I know the fruit of His sanctifying grace will be goodness and mercy all of the days of my life. And when it is all said and done, I will be glorified and spend eternity in Your presence.

—Adapted from Psalm 23

Group Discussion

Key Scripture— Philippians 2:12-13

> Therefore my beloved, as you have always obeyed, not as in my presence only, but now much more in my absence, work out your own salvation with fear and trembling, for it is God who works in you both to will and to do for His good pleasure.

Opening—This is a time of fellowship and sharing about one another's lives.

Prayer—Ask the Lord to make His presence known and to begin the process of transformation into Christlikeness for each participant.

Testimony—Have two or three group members give a testimony of how God is at work in their lives, whether it is through their daily encounters in this study, or some other way.

Discussion Questions:

1. This week's study has focused on the "how" of sanctification. By what means does the Holy Spirit make sanctifying grace available to us? Make sure the group understands grace is more than simply "God's unmerited favor." A good definition of grace is this: "Grace is God's empowering presence that enables us to be who God has called us to be and do what God has called us to do." What are the implications of this definition of grace for those who might claim grace as a license to sin?

2. Discuss Scripture as a means of sanctifying grace. Focus on the quote by Dr. Green where he says, "the Scripture does not merely *tell* about salvation. By the Spirit's grace, the Scripture *works* salvation…"

3. In what ways have group members experienced sanctifying grace as they participate in the life of their local church? What opportunities have they discovered for spiritual fruit to be formed in them?

4. Discuss sacred signs as a means of sanctifying grace. What, if any, sanctifying encounters with the Holy Spirit have group members had during the Lord's Supper, footwashing, or water baptism? Allow 2-3 group members to testify if there is time.

5. Discuss the use of Romans 8:28-29 in this study. Have group members experience a misuse of this text? Does their understanding of it change in light of thinking of it as a "sanctification text?" In what ways have group members experienced sanctifying grace in and "all things" type of encounter with the Holy Spirit?

Yielding to the Spirit

Group members should pair off with someone with whom they feel comfortable sharing. Take a moment to remind them of the Group Covenant, particularly the statement on confidentiality. Practice memorizing the key scripture of the week with one another. Then discuss any personal takeaways that you would like your partner to pray about with you. Conclude this conversation by quietly praying for one another. Be attentive to the leading of the Holy Spirit in the use of spiritual gifts. If you do feel led to share something in this way, ask the group leader to come and witness what is being said. This is to provide a reliable witness for all involved.

DECLARATION OF FAITH

◆◆◆◆◆◆◆

"We Believe....

Holiness to be God's standard of living for His people."

Week 4

Day 1

The Standard of Holiness

DECLARATION OF FAITH

"We Believe....

Holiness to be God's standard of living for His people."

Words to Hide in Your Heart

Pursue peace with all people, and holiness, without which no one will see the Lord (Hebrews 12:14).

Touching Base

There is one particular thing in this final week which needs to be made abundantly clear. Simply put, sanctification is both past and future oriented. Instantaneous cleansing from our sin and depravity in our new birth is the past aspect of sanctification. We never move from this aspect. We are grounded in it. This is the "grace in which we stand" (Romans 5:1-2). We maintain this standing as we moment by moment present ourselves to God as being alive from the dead, and our "members as instruments of righteousness" (Romans 6:13). We only do this as we faithfully respond to the enabling, sanctifying grace of the Holy Spirit.

The future orientation of sanctification is the aspect we need to keep in mind this week. The focus of this aspect of sanctification is not our sin—it is Christ. This aspect is not about suppressing the old nature. It is about being transformed into something new. Our old nature was motivated by the lust of the flesh, the lust of the eye, and the pride of life (1 John 2:16-17). But we are being transformed into people who are motivated by love for God and love for others (Matthew 22:37-40; Mark 12:28-31; Luke 10:25-27). Understanding the difference in these two aspects of sanctification is critical for us if we are to truly be people of holiness.

In a car, you have a rearview mirror and a windshield. The rearview mirror is quite small compared to the windshield. Why is this? Of course, it is because where you are headed is more important to you as the driver than where you have been. If you spend all of your time looking in the rearview mirror, you will eventually crash, harming yourself and others in the process.

This metaphor helps us understand what we are saying about sanctification and holiness. We must remember where we have been. We stand in the grace by which Christ has saved us, cleansed us, and set us free. But our focus must also be on what we are *becoming* as we access the grace in which we stand (Romans 5:2). This is how we are to understand holiness.

With this in mind, we should grasp the idea that holiness is not sin-oriented in its focus. It is Christ-oriented. The focus is not on moral excellence. The focus is on Christlikeness. So when we say holiness is the standard of living for God's people, we are not saying that a particular list of things to avoid or things to do are the standard of living for God's people. We are saying Christlikeness is the standard of living for God's people. That certainly includes moral excellence. But it is so much more!

Searching the Scripture

Read Matthew 5:20

> For I say to you, that unless your righteousness exceeds the righteousness of the scribes and Pharisees, you will be no means enter the kingdom of heaven.

Read 1 Thessalonians 4:7-8

> For God did not call us to uncleanness, but in holiness. Therefore he who rejects this does not reject man, but God, who has also given us His Holy Spirit.

Answer the Following Questions:

1. According to the words of Jesus, our righteousness must exceed whose righteousness?

2. What will happen to us if that fails to be true?

3. To what did God call us?

4. If someone rejects this calling Who is being rejected?

5. Who are we cut off from if we reject God's call to holiness?

Yielding to the Spirit

—Know—

The passages of Scripture we read today make it clear that the calling and expectation of God is for our holiness. If we reject this calling and choose another way, we are rejecting God and the sanctifying Holy Spirit. Jesus warns us what happens to those whose righteousness doesn't exceed the righteousness of the Jewish religious leaders of His day. They kept the very letter of the law. But, in the Sermon on the Mount, which is the context for Jesus' statement, we find that keeping the letter of the law isn't what God is looking for. He wants something much more from us. But the good news of the gospel is that He has done everything necessary to make holiness possible.

These scriptures offer support for article seven of the Church of God Declaration of Faith. There we state our belief that "Holiness is God's standard of living for His people." That is the focus for this entire week.

But we must first understand the concept of a *standard.* A standard is an idea or item that is used as a measure when comparing two things. For example, when we measure something in terms of meters, how do we know what a meter actually is? Is there some agreed upon length that we all use to describe the actual length we call a "meter?" As it turns out there is! The length of a meter is determined to be the distance that light travels in a vacuum in 1/299,792,458 of a second! The speed of light is a constant, which means it does not change. That is why this can be used as a standard.

If holiness is to be our standard by which God measures our lives, it must be an agreed upon, unchanging standard. That standard is not going to be found in a moral code, because there are differences of opinion as to which code is acceptable. Instead, our standard for what is holy is Jesus Christ—the same yesterday, today, and forever (Hebrews 13:8)!

—Be—

There are two extremes in our life when it comes to the ethical and moral choices we make. The first extreme is license—anything goes. The second extreme is legalism—which is excessive focus on a particular moral code. But we are called to freedom in Christ. That is both freedom *from* our past sins and corruption, and freedom *to become* like Jesus in all that we say and do. That is what true liberty looks like.

—Do—

What standard do you use to measure the choices you make in your life? Have you chosen to follow a strict moral code that you inherited or perhaps devised for yourself based on your best understanding of right and wrong? Maybe you have mistakenly used the idea of grace as a license to live any way that feels good and trust in the forgiveness of God. The truth is there is no other way for the Christian to live life besides keeping our eyes on Jesus and allowing Him to guide us in all things. A great side benefit of keeping our eyes on Jesus, is that it becomes impossible to judge anyone else in the process. We only say and do what He tells us to say and do, and that will always be from a place of love. That is what holiness is all about!

Offer a Prayer

Father, I ask that You show me any way in my life that I am measuring myself by anything other than Jesus, the author and perfecter of my faith. Forgive me for judging myself and others wrongly where I have done so. Fill my heart with Your love so that I can be more and more like You in all I think, say, and do. In Jesus name, amen.

Day 2

Becoming Truly Human

Searching the Scripture

Read 1 Corinthians 15:45-49

> And so it is written, "The first man Adam became a living being." The last Adam became a life-giving spirit. However, the spiritual is not first, but the natural, and afterward the spiritual. The first man was of the earth made of dust; the second Man is the Lord from heaven. As was the man of dust, so also are those who are made of dust; and as is the heavenly Man, so also are those who are heavenly. And as we have borne the image of the man of dust, we shall also bear the image of the heavenly Man.

Read 2 Peter 1:2-4

> Grace and peace be multiplied to you in the knowledge of God and of Jesus our Lord, as His divine power has given to us all things that pertain to life and godliness, through the knowledge of Him who called us by glory and virtue, by which have been given to us exceedingly great and precious promises, that through these you may be partakers of the divine nature, having escaped the corruption that is in the world through lust.

Answer the Following Questions:

1. What did the first man Adam become? What did the last Adam become?

2. Who are those that are made of dust like? Who are those that are heavenly like?

3. Whose image will we ultimately bear as the people of God?

Yielding to the Spirit

—*Know*—

Think about your answer this this question:

"Who should we look to as the original example of what it means to truly be human?"

Perhaps your answer was Adam prior to the Fall in the Garden of Eden. If so, your answer was incorrect. You might have thought Adam would be the correct answer because prior to the fall he was sinless, in a right relationship with God, and busy taking care of all that God had given him to do. And that is true. But Adam was not yet everything that God intended for him to become. Adam was innocent, like a child. But to be fully human is more than just being innocent of sin. It is perfect communion with God and all that God has created. The only one who exemplifies that type of humanity is Jesus Christ.

Does it bother you to think of Jesus as human? It shouldn't. Remember that in the incarnation, Jesus revealed God to humanity, but He also revealed humanity to humanity. Jesus showed us an example of what we were to become by grace. That is why we say

Article Seven

holiness equals Christlikeness, and that state of being is God's goal for our sanctification.

—Be—

There are those who might say that being holy and being human have no connection whatsoever. But that is not the case. God's Son took on human form to save us, sanctify us, and ultimately glorify us. Why did He come as a human? Why not something else? It is because humans were made in God's image. It was the perfect means by which to reveal Himself to us and show us what it really means to be human.

—Do—

There are those that say that we have divinity inside of us. We only need to release it to become all that we were meant to be. "Release your inner greatness!" they say. But that is only partly true. Certainly, to be holy is to be fully human, and it is to be everything that God created you to be. But the pathway toward holiness begins with repentance for all the ways we have tried to actualize our humanity on our own without relying on God's grace. And it continues in full reliance on the grace of Jesus Christ, the one who showed us what it truly means to flourish as human beings made in the image of God.

Offer a Prayer

Father, I offer to You my vision of what it means for me to flourish as a human being. Forgive me for the times that I fail to see the connection between holiness and happiness. Align my perspective of what it means to be human with what Jesus modeled for us in His life. Do a work of grace in me so I can follow Him faithfully. In Jesus name, amen.

Day 3

Christ In Me

Searching the Scripture

Read Galatians 2:20-21

> I have been crucified with Christ; it is no longer I who live, but Christ lives in me; and the life which I now live in the flesh I live by faith in the Son of God, who loved me and gave Himself for me. I do not set aside the grace of God; for if righteousness comes through the law, then Christ died in vain.

Read 2 Peter 1:2-4

> Grace and peace be multiplied to you in the knowledge of God and of Jesus our Lord, as His divine power has given to us all things that pertain to life and godliness, through the knowledge of Him who called us by glory and virtue, by which have been given to us exceedingly great and precious promises, that through these you may be partakers of the divine nature, having escaped the corruption that is in the world through lust.

Answer the Following Questions:

1. What does Paul say is true about his life since he has identified with Christ in His crucifixion?

2. How does Paul live his life in the flesh?

3. What would be true if righteousness came by the law?

4. What has God's divine power given to us?

5. What are we able to do through His exceedingly great and precious promises toward us?

6. From what have God's people escaped?

Yielding to the Spirit

—Know—

We are continuing our study this week on the understanding that holiness is God's standard of living for His people. It is crucial that we understand that we are not simply looking to Jesus as a moral example. In other words, holiness is not a result of asking ourselves "what would Jesus do?" If it were, then we might be tempted to be prideful at our ability to live up to His example. Of course, the incarnate Son of God's moral life is an example to us, but He is much more than that. He is the Savior of the world. Because of His sacrifice and His resurrection, we are changed. Something has happened to us because of Him.

Paul describes this something as Christ living in him. Peter describes it as participating in the divine nature. We are not simply inspired by His example, we are indwelt by His very presence! Holiness in our lives is nothing more and nothing less than Christ living out His holy life *through us.* This is our only hope for holiness. We cannot rely on our best understanding of the law to make us holy, or else Christ's death was in vain.

—Be—

Paul says, "it is no longer I who live, but Christ lives in me." But then he continues by saying, "the life which I now live in the flesh I live by faith in the son of God." Which is it? Is Paul no longer living or is he living by faith in the Son of God? The answer is—*both*.

We live by faith in Christ as He lives through us, working to transform our motivations, our very desires, to be like His own—a holy love. But as has been said repeatedly in this study, this only happens as we respond faithfully to the sanctifying grace of the Holy Spirit. We continue to live this human life in this human body with all our passions and desires. Jesus had the same kind of body, but lived victoriously over temptation by the power of the Holy Spirit (see Luke 4, Matthew 4). We must do the same.

—Do—

Is it your goal for Christ's holiness to be lived through your life? What changes might you need to make before this becomes a reality?

Offer a Prayer

Pardon, O gracious Jesus, what I have been;
With Your holy discipline correct what I am.
Direct my life toward what you have created me to be,
And in the end You will be glorified for it all.

—Prayer adapted from *John Wesley's Prayer Journal.*

Day 4

A Holy People

Searching the Scripture

Read Exodus 19:5-6

> "Now therefore, if you will indeed obey My voice and keep My covenant, then you shall be a special treasure to Me above all people; for the earth is Mine. And you shall be to Me a kingdom of priests and a holy nation." These are the words which you shall speak to the children of Israel.

Read 1 Peter 2:9-10

> But you are a chosen generation, a royal priesthood, a holy nation, His own special people, that you may proclaim the praises of Him who called you out of darkness into his marvelous light; who once were not a people but are now the people of God, who had not obtained mercy but now have obtained mercy.

Read Ephesians 2:19-20

> Now, therefore, you are no longer strangers and foreigners, but fellow citizens with the saints and members of the household of God, having been built on the foundation of the apostles and prophets, Jesus Christ

Himself being the chief cornerstone, in whom the whole building, being fitted together, grows into a holy temple in the Lord.

Answer the Following Questions:

1. What were the two requirements God placed on the Israelites?

2. What did God say He wanted the Israelites to be to Him?

3. What did Peter say the special people of God do?

4. What is true of those who were once not a people?

5. What is true of those who had not obtained mercy?

6. Upon what has the household of God been built?

7. Who is the cornerstone of the household of God?

8. What is the whole building growing into?

Yielding to the Spirit

—Know—

No discussion of holiness is complete without considering the fact we are part of something bigger than ourselves. God has always desired to have a people to call His own. A special group of people who would obey His voice and keep covenant with Him.

The special people of God started with Abraham and grew into Israel. Israel failed to keep God's covenant. But Jesus, Himself an Israelite, came and perfectly fulfilled God's law both on Israel's behalf and on behalf of the entire human race. He has made salvation possible for all—not just the Israelites.

Now, God's special people are made up of people from every tribe and tongue. Every ethnicity is represented in God's new family. And God says the same thing to us that He said to Israel—we are a royal priesthood, a holy nation.

It is not just individual Christians who are being sanctified—it is the people of God, the Church! Paul describes the Church as a building that is being built. The cornerstone of this building is Christ. The cornerstone is the first stone that is laid in the foundation and all other stones will be set in reference to it. Jesus is the cornerstone. He is the standard. The standard of holiness!

Like each individual, the Church is not yet what it should be. Paul speaks of it as a building that is growing into a holy temple. One day, the Church will be glorified as the special people of God. Perhaps we see the culmination of Paul's imagery in John's vision of the bride of Christ as the great city descending out of heaven from God (See Revelation 21:9-27).

—Be—

We cannot make the mistake of reducing salvation to something which is only about the individual. God is up to something much bigger. We are part of His special people—His Church. The Holy Spirit is not just sanctifying us as individuals, He is sanctifying the

Church. Being part of that process is not optional. We are born again into a new family.

The Church is holy and is being glorified. The Church is not just another social gathering. It is the temple of the Holy Spirit. It is called to declare the praises of the One who has called us out of darkness and into His marvelous light.

The Church is a demonstration project for God's kingdom. It is to be a place that reflects what it looks like when God is in charge. Like each of us individually, the Church is called to holiness. Like each of us individually, the Church is to be motivated by love for God and love for others.

The Church should be filled with those who love each other well and love the Lord well. Those things that are sources of division for other groups do not divide the people of God. The diversity in God's family is part of its beauty. As Christ lives and loves through each of us toward one another, the Church becomes His body in the world (1 Corinthians 12:12-31). Those who are truly the people of God are known by our love for one another (John 13:35).

—Do—

God has not just called you to be personally conformed to Christlikeness. He has called you to be part of His family, to demonstrate the love of God in tangible ways toward one another and toward the world. Take some time this week to get to know someone in your church family with whom you do not normally visit. Ask questions and listen to their responses. Try to hear what God might be saying in the conversation. See how the Holy Spirit may use this relationship as a means of sanctifying grace for you as individuals and also to strengthen your local church.

Offer a Prayer

Lord, I thank you for the Church. I am grateful You knew we would need to rely on one another, to bear one another's burdens, to encourage one another, and to remind one another of the truth of Your love. Grant to me a work of sanctifying grace to enable me to love my brothers and sisters more deeply and faithfully. Let those in our city see your love expressed in the life of our church. In Jesus name, amen.

Day 5

Holiness On Mission

Searching the Scripture

Read John 17:18-23

> As You sent Me into the world, I also have sent them into the world. And for their sakes I sanctify Myself, that they also may be sanctified by the truth. I do not pray for these alone, but also for those who will believe in Me through their word; that they all may be one, as You, Father, are in Me, and I in You; that they also may be one in Us, that the world may believe that You sent me. And the glory which You gave me I have given them, that they may be one just as We are one: I in them, and You in Me; that they may be made perfect in one, and that the world may know that you have sent Me, and have loved them as You have loved Me.

Read John 20:21

> So Jesus said to them again, "Peace to you! As the Father has sent Me, I also send you."

Answer the Following Questions:

1. Why did Jesus say He was sanctifying Himself?

2. What is Jesus' prayer for His disciples and all who believe in Him through their word?

3. In what way are Jesus' disciples to be one?

4. Why are Jesus' disciples to be one?

5. Why has Jesus given His followers the glory the Father had given to Him?

6. In what way is Jesus sending the church into the world?

Yielding to the Spirit

—Know—

God has been revealing Himself to mankind from the beginning. Scripture tells us that God has spoken to mankind at various times and in various ways (Hebrews 1:1). Paul tells us that one of these ways is through what God has created (Romans 1:20). This is known as "general revelation." God has spoken to us through His inspired Word, first with the Hebrew Scriptures and later through the New Testament writings. We believe these writings are infallible, inspired by the Spirit, and authoritative for our lives as the people of God. The Scriptures themselves point to Jesus (John 5:39). Jesus is the culmination of God's self-revelation. Hebrews says He is the brightness of God's glory and the "express image of His person."

This should help us better understand Jesus' prayer in John 17 more. The glory that the Father had given the Son, the Son is now giving to the Church. And the purpose is for God's people to participate in the divine nature and be one just as the Father and the Son are one. By this loving unity, the world will know Jesus truly did come from God.

Jesus is able to point us to the Father because He is one with the Father. He did nothing without the Father's leadership (John 5:19) and said nothing that the Father had not given Him authority to say (John 12:49). Jesus was sanctified in the sense that His human will was conformed completely to the will of the Father. His purpose was to live out in His body both His love for the Father and His love for the world. Sinless, holy Jesus was the perfect representation of the Father to a lost world. The Church has been given the glory of the Son for the same reason. We too are to be sanctified, fully devoted to embodying holy love for the Father and holy love for one another in order to reveal the loving Father to a lost world.

—Be—

Creation and Scripture continue to reveal God to the world. But the Church is sanctified and filled with the Holy Spirit to engage the world in a way that neither creation or Scripture can. The Spirit uses Scripture to sanctify us, so that holy love can be put on display for the world Jesus gave His life to save. Our sanctification makes us distinct from the world in the sense that we do not share the same motivations, goals, and values. Those that are trapped in the world system are still under the sway of the lust of the flesh, the lust of the eye, and the pride of life. But as the sanctified people of God, our motivation is love for God and love for others. And the "other" is not just our brothers and sisters in the Church. From the perspective of the Church as a whole, the "other" is going to be those that are not yet part of God's family. Our sanctification makes us separate, but it should not isolate us. The sanctified people of God hear our Savior say "Go into all the world and make disciples." Our sanctified response is to yield the totality of our being as an instrument of righteousness by faith in our Savior Jesus Christ and standing in the cleansing and sanctifying grace of the Holy Spirit. At the same time, we willingly yield ourselves to allow Christ to live through us, in service to the Father's will, and in the power of the Holy Spirit.

—Do—

As we conclude the study this week, it is good time for you to review and reflect. What is the Holy Spirit saying to you and His work in your life? What parts of this study have stood out to you as particularly important at this point in your journey toward holiness? As you do this, take this opportunity to specifically pray about those things the Lord shows you. My prayer is that this study might be used as a means of sanctifying grace in your life by the power of the Holy Spirit.

> Now may the God of peace Himself sanctify you completely; and may your whole spirit, soul, and body be

preserved blameless at the coming of our Lord Jesus Christ.

He who calls you is faithful, who also will do it (1 Thessalonians 5:23-24).

Offer a Prayer

In light of what you have learned this week and throughout this entire study, offer a prayer of your own from your heart to God.

Group Discussion

Key Scripture— Hebrews 12:14

> Pursue peace with all people, and holiness, without which no one will see the Lord.

Opening—This is a time of fellowship and sharing about one another's lives.

Prayer—Ask the Lord to make His presence known and to begin the process of transformation into Christ-likeness for each participant.

Testimony—Have two or three group members give a testimony of how God is at work in their lives, whether it is through their daily encounters in this study or some other way.

Discussion Questions:

1. The introduction this week used the example of a windshield and a rearview mirror to talk about holiness and sanctification. Discuss the significance of that metaphor and how it might inform the way we speak of holiness and sanctification after this study.

Group Discussion

2. What does it mean for something to be a standard? With the understanding that holiness is the goal of our sanctification, how do we practically live out the belief that holiness is God's standard of living for His people. How do we make decisions about right and wrong—by looking back at our past, or looking forward at our future? Why?

3. Discuss the difference between Jesus being our moral example ("What would Jesus do?") and Jesus expressing His holiness through our lives. How do we balance this truth out with our responsibility to "yield our members as instruments of righteousness?"

4. Discuss the importance of unity in the Church as an expression of corporate holiness. How does our understanding of holiness as "love for God and love for others" inform what we mean by the term "unity?"

5. The statement was made on day five that holiness means the Church is separate from the world, but not isolated from the world. Discuss what this means practically in terms of the mission of God.

6. What are some ways the Church can reveal God through our love for Him, our love for one another, and by God's love for the world being manifested through us as His people?

Yielding to the Spirit

Group members should pair off with someone with whom they feel comfortable sharing. Take a moment to remind them of the Group Covenant, particularly the statement on confidentiality. Practice memorizing the key scripture of the week with one another. Then discuss any personal takeaways that you would like your partner to pray about with you. Conclude this conversation by quietly praying for one another. Be attentive to the leading of the Holy Spirit in the use of spiritual gifts. If you do feel led to share something in this way, ask the group leader to come and witness what is being said. This is to provide a reliable witness for all involved.

Church of God
Declaration of Faith

We Believe:

1. In the verbal inspiration of the Bible.
2. In one God eternally existing in three persons; namely, the Father, Son, and Holy Ghost.
3. That Jesus Christ is the only begotten Son of the Father, conceived of the Holy Ghost, and born of the Virgin Mary. That Jesus was crucified, buried, and raised from the dead. That He ascended to heaven and is today at the right hand of the Father as the Intercessor.
4. That all have sinned and come short of the glory of God and that repentance is commanded of God for all and necessary for forgiveness of sins.
5. That justification, regeneration, and the new birth are wrought by faith in the blood of Jesus Christ.
6. In sanctification subsequent to the new birth, through faith in the blood of Christ; through the Word, and by the Holy Ghost.
7. Holiness to be God's standard of living for His people.
8. In the baptism with the Holy Ghost subsequent to a clean heart.

9. In speaking with other tongues as the Spirit gives utterance and that it is the initial evidence of the baptism of the Holy Ghost.

10. In water baptism by immersion, and all who repent should be baptized in the name of the Father, and of the Son, and of the Holy Ghost.

11. Divine healing is provided for all in the atonement.

12. In the Lord's Supper and washing of the saints' feet.

13. In the premillennial second coming of Jesus. First, to resurrect the righteous dead and to catch away the living saints to Him in the air. Second, to reign on the earth a thousand years.

14. In the bodily resurrection; eternal life for the righteous, and eternal punishment for the wicked.